SPEAK OUT

Kathy DeGraw

SPEAK OUT

Releasing *the* **POWER** *of*
DECLARING PRAYER

CREATION
HOUSE

Library of Congress Control Number: 2017937196
International Standard Book Number: 978-1-62999-217-4
E-book International Standard Book Number:
978-1-62999-218-1

First edition

17 18 19 20 21 — 987654321
Printed in the United States of America

THIS BOOK IS DEDICATED TO:

My family, for faithfully standing by
me and enduring as I prayed out loud,
declared in the midst of a conversation,
and spoke to everything and anything,
whether or not it had ears to hear;

Everyone who stood by me in faith and
contributed in the natural and spiritual to
the manifestation of my Dodge Charger
so that the world could see the power of
decreeing and declaring through prayer.

CONTENTS

Introduction xi

1: Praying Versus Declaring 1

2: Spoken Words Have Power 25

3: God Spoke and Created 63

4: Jesus Spoke, and Things Responded 83

5: Does Your Faith Line Up? 105

6: Scriptures Were Meant to Be Read. 123

7: Lord, You Said If I Ask. 141

8: Renewing Your Mind 169

9: Everything in Order 185

10: Defining Your Words 209

11: Writing a Declaration 221

12: Taking the Territory 239

13: Audible Instructions 259

Epilogue. 271

Notes 272

About the Author. 274

Additional Books by Kathy DeGraw. 275

Contact the Author 276

Introduction
OPENING PROPHETIC DECLARATION

I decree this is a new day, a new season for you.

I call forth the abundance of heaven to rain down upon you.

I declare that this day the revelation of declaring and decreeing will open to you, that knowledge will be in abundance, and the Spirit of the Lord would bring forth understanding.

I say and declare that the spirit of understanding and wisdom will be upon you.

I release good and abundant knowledge to come through this time of learning and growing in your prayer life.

I declare an ease of receiving the revelation the Holy Spirit desires to impart.

I call forth every good and perfect thing the Lord wants you to receive. In Jesus' name, amen!

1
PRAYING VERSUS DECLARING

PRAYER IS INTIMACY, silence, solitude, and connecting with the Father, spirit to Spirit. We develop a relationship with Him by spending time with Him. In our time in the presence of God we receive revelation from our Father. It comes in as an impartation and deposit as a result of putting ourselves in a position to receive from Him, our Creator. However, once all that information is received, what do you do with it?

Declaring and decreeing is putting out and calling forth what you received through prayer. It distributes out through the power of your words what you received in prayer. Declaring is activating your faith and creating movement in the natural based on the revelation you received. It is taking everything you received from the Father in that quiet place and releasing it to establish the kingdom and break down strongholds.

I like to say that prayer is where we take in from the Father, and declaring is where we put out what we received from the Father. They are both equally important.

I received a prophetic word years ago that said that I would change the way the church prayed. The exact word was, "My daughter, you have a desire for prayer. You've been thinking, 'Lord, I feel like the church has forgotten about prayer. I wish someone would reinstitute prayer in the house.' Guess who I am going to use? I'm going to use you to rally men and women to seek Me, seek Me, seek Me, like they have never before." When I received this word I thought to myself, "This word is so far off." I took the prophetic word and put it up on a shelf. I thought, "I have no desire to teach the church how to pray." Years later as I was writing a book the Holy Spirit got a hold of me, and it felt as though a bolt of lightning shot down throughout my body. He brought me back to this prophetic word and reminded me that I had been speaking out of my mouth for the past six months that people didn't know how to pray. It was then that I received the revelation that reminded me that the church is not a building but the people. I embraced my calling to teach people how to pray.

My first desire in teaching people how to pray was to teach them how to pray out loud. I don't think I have ever heard one sermon on the power of praying aloud. In fact, I know that when the moment comes to pray aloud over the offering or for a sick person everyone is hoping that it won't be them who is asked to pray. It is similar to what happens at the dinner table or at a small-meal blessing while being out with a friend; usually we sit back and wait for someone else to pray so that we don't have to. One person, usually the pastor or ministry leader, is always looked on to pray. Even when the leader of the group chirps up and asks someone to pray before they are called upon, nobody wants to be chosen.

When you are asked to pray aloud, many thoughts can run through your head. "Is it going to sound good enough?" "Who is listening?" "I have no idea what to pray!" People feel inadequate in their prayer life. People feel insecure and intimidated about praying out loud when they hear how others pray out loud. When you go into a prayer meeting or hear another person pray out loud and the anointing is really flowing from that person, you think to yourself, "That person can really pray." You don't stop to consider that the anointing that is flowing through them is directly from the Holy Spirit, and the same anointing that is flowing through them can flow through you. Instead, people use that as an opportunity to make up excuses, such as, "I can't pray like that; I don't have the words to say," or, "I have thoughts but don't know how to put them all together in a prayer." People cower back and never try to pray aloud out of fear of failure. You can't fail when you pray! The Holy Spirit is right there interceding and co-laboring with you, and Jesus takes all of our prayers up to heaven and makes them sweet incense before the Father.

The Holy Spirit takes part when we pray. We can start praying in the natural from what we know, but as we continue to pray the anointing takes over. When the anointing comes upon us, all of a sudden prayer just becomes easy. We start receiving what I call *downloads*. Thoughts rapidly start dropping in our mind and spirit of what we should be praying for and what words to say. This is the Spirit of God co-laboring with our prayers, which are sometimes weak and ineffective. As we go forward in faith and attempt to pray, the Holy Spirit will pray with us. He desires to take part with us when we pray and make effectual intercession before the throne of God.

In Romans 8:27 it says, "Now He who searches the hearts knows what the mind of the Spirit is, because He makes intercession for the saints according to the will of God." He who searches the mind is Christ, and Christ knows the mind of the Spirit. Jesus makes intercession for us (Rom. 8:34). We have such power with the Holy Spirit and Jesus on our side to make intercession and co-labor with us. What we need to do is trust and rely on them co-laboring with us. We need to do our part to open our mouths and speak out and pray. We cannot leave it to them alone; we have a part to play in it. We need to participate. There are many Christians who don't want to participate in prayer. They ask people to intercede for them, but they don't want to open their mouths and pray for themselves. They have the greatest weapon, the Spirit of God Himself, who co-labors with them!

So, then, what is the difference between praying in our mind silently and declaring out of our mouth, verbally?

Prayer can take on different forms. The most common type of prayer is when we communicate with God in our mind. This is us asking God to protect our families, help us find a job, and other simple requests that we make known to God. The majority of us have been taught to pray in our mind, communicating with God. We can and do hear from God when we pray. But most of us think it is our own thoughts and don't recognize it as the voice of the Lord giving us discernment. (To learn more about hearing from God read my book *Flesh, Satan or God: Who Are You Hearing From?*)

You can pray through a time of solitude and silence, which we call meditation. You hear from God during this time, but you are not speaking out loud back to God. You are communicating silently in your mind. You are receiving, yet in a different way. It is a great time of focusing your attention on God and getting into a quiet place to find rest and solace. I start every day in a time of solitude with the Lord and literally cannot go through my day without it. If for some reason I have to jump out of bed to attend to a need, as soon as that situation is taken care of I go to my secret place. At the beginning of the day, I sit in solitude for fifteen minutes to gather my thoughts, quiet my soul, and connect with my Father spirit to Spirit.

People pray in the spirit, or in tongues, as another way of praying. The Holy Spirit has given us a very incredible prayer language to pray to release those things that we don't know how to pray during spiritual warfare, or any time. Praying in the spirit is powerful, impactful, and produces results! The Holy Spirit co-labors with us in this time of prayer. Even though the Spirit is releasing on our behalf, we still need to co-labor with Him, and that is why we have the power to declare.

Prayer declarations are times when we are speaking things into existence with power and authority. This binds and restricts demonic forces. There are many things we can declare and decree for, such as salvation, marriage, or a new job. We can bind and restrict the demonic realm from activating in our lives, bind spirits of offense from operating against us, and command sickness and disease to go in Jesus' name.

"Faith comes by hearing" (Rom. 10:17), and as we speak aloud what we want to see manifest or take authority over, it will increase our faith. Several times a day we are impacted by what people say, either positively or negatively. It impacts us and affects our mood. What if we could change our emotions and attitude by what we pray aloud? There is power in speaking out! Jesus said in Luke 10:19,

"Behold, I give you the authority to trample on serpents and scorpions, and over all the power of the enemy, and nothing shall by any means hurt you." When we speak out words in advance on the offense of a situation and bind and restrict spiritual warfare on the defense, nothing by any means shall hurt us.

One time I was ministering at a church about the power of decreeing. I started to declare aloud in prayer. What I was doing appeared very foreign to the congregation. They had never heard of declaring and had never been taught to declare. I want you to think about the prayers that haven't been answered or the warfare you have experienced in your situation that hasn't stopped. If you were taught to pray differently or declare, would you have seen the manifestation of your petition? The church, we the people, must rise up and fight and pray differently to see the fruit of our prayers. Speak out with authority into the spirit realm what you want to see happen in the natural realm. Take authority and command the spirit realm to activate on your words. It changed my life, and I want to empower you to have it change yours!

Praying the same repetitive prayers can get you into a mentality of defeat. There are times when you can feel stagnant praying your prayer list. Is there authority or faith in consistently repeating a list that you are not enthusiastic about? You are simply doing your duty. Declaring takes action and activation! When you rise up, take your authority, and get your physical body moving in alignment with your prayers of declaration, all of a sudden there is an atmosphere shift within you. Your prayer time becomes enthusiastic. Heaven responds to your actions and faith to believe and receive!

Empower your prayer life by decreeing and declaring. When you do, you are establishing and taking the authority that Jesus gave to you. You go from wondering if God can or will do it to speaking it into existence and co-laboring with the very Spirit of God! Empower yourself! Do something for yourself that you would normally ask another Christian to do for you. Speak out on your own behalf! Declare and prophesy into your own situation! Get active in your walk with the Lord. Open your Bible and deeply digest God's Word. When you empower yourself, the enemy loses his foothold and discovers that you are serious for the kingdom!

Declaring charges the atmosphere around you. When you start to declare things that you know in the natural and keep declaring them, the Holy Spirit will arise within you and start giving you further revelation about what else to declare. When you receive discernment and co-labor with the Holy Spirit your prayer time ignites, and you become excited to pray! What kingdom impact Christians could make if we all started speaking to everything and every condition! Speak out with your words in your prayer time.

Power and authority from the very Spirit of God are inside you! That means when your declaration is in alignment with God's will and purposes for your life, it will manifest! Jesus didn't go to the grave so that you wouldn't take your authority. He transferred His authority to you! What if all Christians decreed and declared for five, ten, or fifteen minutes a day? What could change? Would people be delivered, the homeless fed and sheltered, the abused healed, our churches filled? What dreams would come true? Could marriages be restored and financial situations turned around? What if everyone spent fifteen minutes a day declaring what they desire instead of talking and complaining about what they don't have? I believe heaven and Earth's atmosphere would be impacted, and a shift would happen in the world.

Declaring isn't a "name it, claim it" game. You take a biblical fact, a word of knowledge, or a revelation that the Father has given you, and activate your faith. Put authoritative words with it to call the spirit realm into action! There is a difference between naming and claiming and believing and receiving. We don't go around loosely naming and claiming. We are speaking with the authority that Christ gave us. Christ transferred to us the gifts and callings that our Father already had planned for us.

I'm not one of those name it, claim it preachers who encourage everyone to speak out and declare what they want to manifest. I am a preacher who is trying to teach people how to pray differently, according to faith. When in alignment with God's will, anything can manifest in our lives. I teach people the opposite of the "name it, claim it" preachers. I teach them to proceed with caution and always emphasize that whatever they are calling forth has to be in accordance with God's will.

What about declaring some good things to come forth and manifest in your life? Declaring is to speak out and reveal something in the spiritual to cause it to happen in the natural. It is to proclaim out and speak out with words in order to get a response. Declaring can include releasing some positive thoughts out of your mouth at the beginning of the day. It can include claiming and taking territory over your day and releasing your expectations for the day, such as:

I declare I am going to be happy, joyful, and full of God's love today, demonstrating God's love to all I encounter.

I declare my marriage to be restored, and I call forth unity, love, and restoration.

I declare my body is going to feel great today, and I will be full of strength to accomplish God's work.

I declare I am going to have favor in the sight of the Lord and with man today.

Call forth is a term you can use when making simple statements. Calling forth indicates that you are expecting a result to happen from a verbal command you speak out. Calling forth is what Jesus did to the fig tree. He summoned it into action and told it, "Let no fruit grow on you ever again" (Matt. 21:19). I am sure there are things in your life that could stand to be called forth, such as:

I call forth a good Christian job to come my way where I will have influence and favor in the marketplace.

I call forth my loved ones to come into a relationship with Jesus Christ.

I call forth doors to open on my behalf where I can share my talents, giftings, and love of the Lord.

The word *command* is another powerful word to speak out in our prayer time. Jesus commanded the demons to get out of the man and go into the swine, as in Matthew 8:32: "And He said to them, 'Go.' So when they had come out, they went into the herd of swine. And suddenly the whole herd of swine ran violently down the steep place into the sea, and perished in the water." He said, "Go." Go is a command. What do you need to speak into the atmosphere and tell to go in your life? We can take authority over the spiritual realm and tell things to go, such as:

> *I command sickness and disease in my body to go in Jesus' name.*
>
> *I command no delays in my God-given assignments. Hindrances go in Jesus' name.*
>
> *I command distractions in my life to go in Jesus' name.*
>
> *I command everything unproductive and unfruitful to go now in the name of Jesus!*

Declare, call forth, and command, whether you are activating something positive to come forth or binding and restricting a negative spiritual warfare attack. You don't always have the time or opportunity to pray. I know this may sound like an odd statement coming from a minister, but in emergency situations or certain ministry situations you don't have time to go into your prayer closets. It is in these moments that coupling the faith we have in our soul with the power of declaring results in quick, effectual, meaningful prayer that can change the outcome of an immediate situation.

When in an emergency situation sometimes all you have time for is to shout out the name of Jesus. In highly intense situations we can forget how to pray or be in such a moment of trauma that we are more concerned with what's going to happen in the immediate moment. We are in shock and freeze up and don't know what to do in the situation. I am sure some of you have heard of people calling on the name of Jesus as a rapist was about to attack them, as a child was about to get in an accident, as a robber was approaching them, and at other times where violent attacks, crimes, or accidents were threatening them. When confronted with a situation such as this, would you remember to call on the name of Jesus? Or would you freeze up and forget what to do?

When I heard people I knew talking about how they called on the name of Jesus I too wanted that faith. I purposed in my heart and set in my mind to do the same if ever needed. I knew I wanted to be able to call out the name of Jesus and have that be enough to save me if I ever were in a situation where danger was imminent. But, when actually confronted with such a situation, would I, could I, actually do it? I was not certain that I would remember to do it. When confronted with immediate danger, you don't have time to pray. God's Word tells us to speak to our mountain (Matt. 21:21) and that "death and life are in the power of the tongue" (Prov. 18:21). When we study God's Word it teaches us about the out-spoken Word of God. It instructs us what to say. It is the words we speak out that are powerful. The strongest word that we can possibly speak out is the name of Jesus. One word! One name, the name of our Lord and Savior!

In Proverbs 18:10 we read, "The name of the Lord is a strong tower; the righteous run to it and are safe." The name of Jesus saves. He saves not just as our Deliverer and Redeemer but as our Protector (Ps. 91). I love to study the Complete Jewish Bible. I often think, "I am going to go and see how this verse reads in that translation." In the Complete Jewish Bible this verse reads, "The name of Adonai is a strong tower; a righteous person runs to it and is raised high [above danger]." "High above danger" is so true to what I have experienced.

Some time ago my question of whether or not I would remember to call on the name of Jesus in a dire circumstance was answered when I had one of those moments. I had one of those moments in my life where it was all I could do just to shout out the name of Jesus and speak into the atmosphere to dispatch angelic warrior-servants on assignment. My team member Carolyn and I found ourselves driving in treacherous road conditions on the way to a ministry trip in Nebraska. We couldn't turn back because even though we weren't far along in the trip the roads behind us were worse than the roads ahead. Carolyn and I had never driven in conditions that bad in the thirty years we had been driving. We were driving on snow and ice with blowing winds and poor visibility. Snow was coming down so hard at one point that we had to pull off of the road for a couple of hours. We were driving on the highway and it was still rapidly snowing when all of a sudden a semi started to jackknife right in front of us. The road conditions were such that slamming on the brakes was not an option. As we saw this semi turning sideways on the highway and spreading out over all three lanes in front of us we did not know if we would be able to stop in time and miss hitting him. We knew we were in trouble and started shouting out the name of Jesus. We didn't pray! We didn't have time to pray, "Oh, Father, please save us. Come to your children," etc. I am not saying that there is anything wrong with praying. I do pray daily. In this case, we didn't have time to pray. We had time to call on the name of Jesus, like a strong tower, to run into and be saved (Prov. 18:10)! Carolyn decreed the words, "God protect us."

There was a parked police car on the side of the highway, and the semi was headed right for the driver's door, with the police officer in his car. All of a sudden I called out, "I send angels to that police car right now in the name of Jesus." As those angels went forth and the name of Jesus was being released into the atmosphere, suddenly, to our complete amazement, we saw something supernatural. The semi, which was partially jackknifed and directly in front of us, completely straightened out and missed the police car, which was only two feet away. Carolyn was able to maintain complete control of the van, while each vehicle—ours, the semi, and the police car—went on its way, straightened out. Therefore there was no accident, no damage, and no one even stopped. The name of Jesus lifted us high above danger! Praise God!

The name of Jesus does raise us high above danger when we call out His name! I believe that I was able to call out the name of Jesus in that incident because I knew the power of Jesus' name. I have heard stories and testimonies of the power of His name. I have read books on my identity in Christ. I have also read A. L. Gill's book *Destined for Dominion* on power and authority (available on my website, www.degrawministries.org). It speaks of our authority in the name of Jesus.

He has transferred His power of attorney to me! That's right! Jesus died and descended to hell for me, and on the third day He arose and ascended into heaven. His Word says in Luke 10:19, "Behold, I give you the authority to trample on serpents and scorpions, and over all the power of the enemy, and nothing shall by any means hurt you." He has given me power and authority! He has given you power and authority! We have to know the power and authority that we have been given in His name. Just like a person who is in the world gives someone power of attorney to make decisions and act on their behalf, Jesus Christ has given us power of attorney and power and authority to operate in His name.

The name of Jesus heals, sets free, saves, delivers, and much more. The name of Jesus can cast out a demon! It can take an evil spirit that has invaded someone's life and force it to disembody the person. It is a miracle to be able to cast a demon out of a person. That is the power of Jesus' name! The power of His name creates miracles!

Knowing the name of Jesus, the power and authority it holds, and how we are to use it comes from knowing our identity in Christ. You must know who you are in Christ. You must know that you are valuable. You must know that you are of the kingdom. You are from a world that cannot be shaken. In Acts 2:25 it says, "For David says concerning Him: 'I foresaw the LORD always before my face, For He is at my right hand, that I may not be shaken.'" We must know the name and power of Jesus. We must know our authority! There will be times in our lives when we will need to draw upon His name.

Jesus instructed us to speak to our mountain: "For assuredly, I say to you, whoever says to this mountain, 'Be removed and be cast into the sea,' and does not doubt in his heart, but believes that those things he says will be done, he will have whatever he says" (Mark 11:23). In this verse He talks about the power of speaking to our mountains and having belief. He instructs us to *say*. To *say* means "to utter" aloud or "to express in words." When we are in prayer there must be times when we are praying aloud to our heavenly Father.

The Bible says, "Death and life are in the power of the tongue, And those who love it will eat its fruit" (Prov. 18:21). We can talk all day long to people, but when it comes to using our authority and speaking aloud to the spiritual atmosphere and our heavenly Father too often the church fails to embrace that death and life are truly in the power of the tongue.

Jesus spoke to things! He spoke to a fig tree: "And seeing a fig tree by the road, He came to it and found nothing on it but leaves, and said to it, 'Let no fruit grow on you ever again.' Immediately the fig tree withered away" (Matt. 21:19). The fig tree responded to what He said. Imagine if some of the things that we have been praying for silently suddenly manifested if we started praying and speaking to them aloud. If we haven't seen things manifest naturally, is it going to hurt to change the way we pray and to try to pray differently?

Jesus modeled how to declare when He taught the disciples the Lord's Prayer.

> In this manner, therefore, pray: Our Father in heaven, Hallowed be Your name. Your kingdom come. Your will be done On earth as it is in heaven. Give us this day our daily bread. And forgive us our debts, As we forgive our debtors. And do not lead us into temptation, But deliver us from the evil one. For Yours is the kingdom and the power and the glory forever. Amen.
> —MATTHEW 6:9-13

You should pray like this: Our Father in heaven, help us to honor your name. Come and set up

> your kingdom, so that everyone on earth will
> obey you, as you are obeyed in heaven. Give
> us our food for today. Forgive us for doing
> wrong, as we forgive others. Keep us from being
> tempted and protect us from evil.
>
> —Matthew 6:9-13, cev

The Lord's Prayer is full of statements that command. When you diagram this prayer it is full of commitment, praise, spiritual reign, God's will and purpose, deliverance, protection, and much more, all being declarations of what we are petitioning the Father to do.

When declaring we are speaking into existence, believing what has already happened in the spiritual realm. Jesus died for us over two thousand years ago. When He died He purchased our healing and deliverance. The Word of God says by His stripes we are healed (1 Pet. 2:24). When we are declaring we are acknowledging what He has done for us and calling it into existence, similar to when He purchased our healing. We know He died for us. We know that we can live a life of victory. Therefore we speak into existence something that He already has done for us. In heaven God's plans are written for our lives. By declaring, we desire those written plans not only to manifest in the spiritual but to be accomplished in the natural.

In some instances all we have time to do is to declare out or prophetically speak into a person quickly. I do street evangelism, and one portion of my ministry is sharing God's love. I call it "Be Love." Being love is serving God and people and loving people in each and every moment. Every encounter with another person should be a divine encounter to share God's love.

Store and restaurant evangelism is one of the ways I share the love of God. Each time I am out in public I put away my phone and discern for prophetic encounters. Putting away my phone means that while I am waiting in the checkout lane to pay or while I am being helped in a store, having fabric or meat cut, for example, I don't use that time to check my e-mails or social media. I use that time to speak light and life into a person. A person may not receive it if you ask, "Can I pray for you right here, right now?" However, if we speak out simple declarations over their life they will feel edified and encouraged. I speak statements such as:

> *Have a great day, and may God's blessing, love, and favor be in abundance in your life today.*

> *I speak health and healing into your body right now in the name of Jesus.*

> *I call forth the prosperity of heaven to open on your behalf with every good and perfect thing for your life.*

> *I command angels to go forth and activate on your behalf.*

These simple declarations are statements of faith that you impart into someone. When statements are declarations and establishments spoken over someone's life it increases their faith and changes their day and possibly even their attitude about the situation they are facing. When you make these simple declarations people believe in the things that you have just spoken. Offense will not rise awkward opportunity for them to be prayed over occurred, and you just spoke light and life into them. We don't have the chance to take a cashier's hand and pray for them while people are waiting in a line. In rare cases we can, but most people who are bold enough to do that don't know how to cut the prayer short enough, and they pray longer than they should while a person is working. By speaking simple, scriptural declarations into a person's life we are praying for them, just in a different way. With the simple statements that you have just spoken over a person you very well could be assisting them to establish something in their life. As you have just spoken out over them, you have also given them an idea of what they could be speaking out over themselves. You can even end your time together by saying, "OK, now go and speak this out over the situation several times a day."

Each time I see a person I try to make a conscious effort to declare over them, even if it is as simple as saying, "Have a blessed day." I truly believe that when I speak that over a person a declaration of blessing is being released into their day. There is power in the words we speak. Why just say good-bye when we can speak blessings into someone's day?

Declaring can be quoting out Scripture. The Bible is full of simple statements and commands that are declarations. These scriptures state facts about the good things that we call forth. These scriptures tell us what our inheritance is and assist us in binding and restricting evil spirits. As you learn about declarations and what they consist of you will start reading the Bible differently. As you are reading you will be able to pull out the declarations. I even underline them in my Bible in a certain color so that while preaching or in an intense situation where I need to get to them in a hurry they stand out to me, and I can start declaring at a moment's notice. I will discuss the power of declaring Scripture more in another chapter.

We ask others to pray for us more than we pray for ourselves. If people knew the power of declaring they would be able to take hold of their situation and stop seeking others for prayer. One of the common concerns I have is when you ask someone to pray for you, how do you know they are actually going to do it? How do you know how long they are going to pray and what they are going to pray? Are they going to pray with passion, power, and authority? Do they really know how to engage in spiritual warfare and fight and pray for you? Are they simply praying out of obligation and passivity? Are their prayers effective? Are they shooting up a quick bullet prayer, or are they truly sitting down and interceding for you? Do you know who they truly are? Is intercession their gift or your perception of their gift? Just because someone on social media or in a church meeting "knows how to pray" doesn't mean that they know how to pray for you. If they are not passionate about your situation they may not pray one single prayer for you. Meanwhile, you asked them to pray, and you didn't take authority yourself. Your prayer didn't get answered, or your situation wasn't changed. You don't know what someone else is or is not praying for you. That is why it is so important that you take responsibility for your own prayer life. You don't know what another person is praying for you. That is why I am so passionate about encouraging you to pray for yourself. Did you ever stop to think that your prayer request is not their responsibility and prayer burden to take on? Yes, that is exactly right; hard to hear maybe, but right.

We are not all called to take on each other's prayer responsibility. Think of it this way. The large ministries take in thousands of prayer requests a week. The founders of these organizations usually cannot pray for all of those individuals on a daily basis. Yes, they may lay their hands on the request and call things forth in faith. I'm sure there are some prayers that get answered. But do you want to be a part of some prayers answered, or do you want to take authority over your situation and know that something is being declared into the atmosphere each and every day? Even smaller ministries can put up a quick bullet prayer as the request comes in. But when does that prayer request become obligation because you asked them versus heartfelt passion because it was their burden to pray? Some may say that if we are going to be love, then we should pray for every single request that comes in. Well, I'm sure most ministries do that by quickly laying their hands on a pile of cards or reaching out to the screen on their laptop. But is that the kind of prayer you really want? No! You want someone who is going to tear up hell and call down heaven. That person can and will be you.

Listen to the instructions from the Holy Spirit on how to pray. Read this book and put it into practical application. Seek your deliverance so that there is no passivity or complacency hindering your prayer life. Learn your identity and authority as a believer so that you know your prayer has power and effectual results (James 5:16). You have power and authority; you just need to unleash what is already within you. The kingdom of God is within you. You have to release it out of you!

People would rather have a "prayer warrior" pray over their request than take the issue themselves to the Father, but the truth about prayer is that you have more power praying for your request than another person has. God said, "I give you authority." It is your situation. Did you ever think that your request isn't manifesting because it is your responsibility to pray? Stop asking people to pray, and start taking responsibility for your prayer life.

You have to get to the point where you take responsibility for your own prayer issues. It is not everyone's responsibility to pray for you. They have their own prayer burdens and what the Spirit is prompting them to pray for in that season. People want others to pray for them more than they want to rise up and take authority and speak and decree for their own situation! There is more power in you taking authority and declaring over your situation than there is for another person to pray for you.

> You will also declare a thing, And it will be established for you; So light will shine on your ways.
>
> —Job 22:28

> I shall not die, but live, And declare the works of the Lord.
>
> —Psalm 118:17

Until we know our full authority, and even afterward, there are times when we may want to choose when to pray out loud and when to pray silently in our minds. In spiritual warfare we need to be careful. I definitely believe that there are times when we should not speak into the atmosphere. When we look at the Scriptures, it was after Jesus was baptized in the water and the Spirit of the Lord descended upon Him like a dove that the Father said, "This is my beloved Son, in whom I am well pleased" (Matt. 17:5). When this happened the devil saw and heard the declaration. When the Spirit took Jesus out in the desert the devil came and tempted Him. The devil activated on the out-spoken word and prophetic proclamation by the Father. There will be times in our lives when we should keep our activities and prayers silent in order to leave no room for the enemy to activate on them. As I was writing this book, in fact, the Father told me not to speak out that I was writing a book. I simply called this a special project I was working on. He instructed me that if I spoke out that I was writing a book and the topic of which I was writing there would be much more warfare. Because of this warning I kept silent out of obedience to the Father.

Once we know our full authority and identity in Christ and know how to war, decree, and declare, then I don't think we have to be as aware of what we do or don't speak out. If we speak out something that we should have kept silent, we simply decree against the enemy coming and attacking what we spoke out. We can annihilate the demonic spiritual realm once we know how.

When should we pray scriptural verses? What should we declare or decree? This can be a personal decision and your very own conviction from the Holy Spirit. In order to assist some of you who are in the initial process of attempting to figure this out I will try to outline my recommendations. Please remember these are just suggestions. You ultimately need to yield to the Holy Spirit and listen to His direction. If you need to learn more about hearing from God and discernment, see my book *Flesh, Satan, or God: Who Are You Hearing From?*

PRAY FOR:

- Salvation: You don't want the enemy to hear you pray out loud for the salvation of a loved one. Otherwise, he may begin to spiritually attack them.

- Ministry opportunities: Pray and seek the Father for opportunities to be love and expand His kingdom. Pray for divine appointments and open doors of invitation to preach the gospel.

DECLARE FOR:

- Physical healing: Speak aloud to your body parts and tell them to work right, be recreated, and to come into alignment with the will of God and the perfection with which you were made in your mother's womb.

- Finances: Speak to your bills and debt and command them to be paid. Call forth finances to increase, a good steady job, and unexpected money to come your way.

DECREE FOR:

- Spiritual warfare attacks: Decree aloud into the spiritual atmosphere for the enemy to be bound and restricted, that he will not attack you in Jesus' name.

- Command demonic beings to get out of your life and away from your family.

What is the difference between declaring and decreeing? Declaring is to call positive things forth and into existence. What we need has already happened in the spirit realm. We are taking ownership of what the Father war to release to us and saying it in a strong and confider as though it already exists. While speaking out, declaring it to be absolute, making it clear and evident, as in an official announcement.

Decreeing instructs evil powers to be bound and restricted. When we are decreeing, we are giving an official order with authority and instructing evil spirits what to do. When we rebuke evil powers we claim our authority in Christ, since *rebuke* means "to take authority over the enemy." However, when we take authority over them we do so by instructing them with a follow-up command of what to do. An example would be, "I command evil powers to leave this region." You are taking authority by commanding but then giving them an instruction of what to do.

Nearly everyone operates in some position of authority in some part of their life. As bosses, parents, or leaders we make requests and issue commands daily. We give instructions to people and desire to force them to come into alignment with our opinions and way of doing things. Yet, when it comes to directing and ordering the spirit realm around us we are silent. You have authority! You are placed and positioned with an inheritance! Speak to what is important and hold your tongue when you should. Rise up and change your situation!

2
SPOKEN WORDS
HAVE POWER

THERE IS POWER in the words we speak. Our mouth can speak blessings into people and truly encourage them and change their attitude toward the day they are having. Our mouth can also speak negativity, belittlement, and anger. When our mouths speak negative things toward another person, he or she can become upset, depressed, or hurt. When our words to someone about another person are gossip, triangulation, or slander it will affect the emotions of the person we are speaking to. They could leave the conversation and go from having a good day to feeling heavy because of what was just spoken to them.

James speaks of the power we have available in our mouth.

> Indeed, we put bits in horses' mouths that they may obey us, and we turn their whole body. Look also at ships: although they are so large and are driven by fierce winds, they are turned by a very small rudder wherever the pilot desires. Even so the tongue is a little member and boasts great things. See how great a forest

a little fire kindles! And the tongue is a fire, a
world of iniquity. The tongue is so set among
our members that it defiles the whole body, and
sets on fire the course of nature; and it is set on
fire by hell.

—James 3:3-6

The tongue can really be used to demolish and destroy
things. It is a powerful weapon, and when we think about
it most of our emotional issues stem from someone
speaking something into our lives. The enemy uses people
to destroy us through words. When a person is not careful
and guarded with their tongue it can create years of pain
for another person.

James goes on to tell us how unruly our tongue is but
that blessing also can proceed out of our mouth.

But no man can tame the tongue. It is an unruly
evil, full of deadly poison. With it, we bless our
God and Father, and with it we curse men, who
have been made in the similitude of God. Out of
the same mouth proceed blessing and cursing.
My brethren, these things ought not to be so.

—James 3:8-10

Blessing comes forth from our mouth! With the same
tongue we curse or ignite people. You need to make a
choice regarding what you are going to do with your
tongue. Are you going to have it be unruly and negative,
or are you going to use it to sing praises to your God,
speaking out blessings over people and calling things that
are not into existence through the power of declaring?

There is much power in the simple words and prayers
we pray out. Declaring out words and statements is not
simply for the future but for immediate results. When

we speak out we can and will see results when we speak out by faith. As I've discussed throughout this book, it is important to speak out what is in accordance with the will of God. How do you know what the will of God is? By spending quiet time with Him.

One of the ways I spend quiet time with Him is when I get up in the morning. Before getting out of bed in the morning I sit in quiet solitude and simply reflect on the Lord. I don't pray, but lie there quietly and listen. I listen for His still, small voice. During this time of listening I am preparing my soul for the day. It gives me a chance to wake up and connect my spirit to His Spirit.

While in this solitary time that I call prayer time I can hear from the Lord simple words, instructions, and directions, or He can lead me in a specific direction in which to pray.

One morning as I was meditating in this way I heard the following in my spirit: "Give me favor, unexpected blessings, and help me reach people far and wide." I repeatedly kept hearing these words in my spirit and then started speaking them out in prayer. Repeatedly, for fifteen to twenty minutes, I kept speaking out in a normal tone, "God, give me favor, unexpected blessings, and help me reach people far and wide." I prayed as the Spirit of the Lord led me. I prayed and spoke out the words the Spirit told me to pray. When we spend time with Him, He will lead and guide us in prayer. I prayed those words until I felt the Spirit of the Lord release me to pray in a different direction.

I started going about my day, and within an hour I started experiencing the manifestation of my declaration prayer.

My executive director brought in love gifts to everyone in the office. We are consistently giving items away in the community and during prophetic evangelism. She felt a quickening in her spirit to purchase items for her fellow team members and to show love to them.

A person we consistently were ministering to called to volunteer that day for our ministry; that definitely was a blessing.

A pastor from another country contacted me to help them establish an inner healing and deliverance ministry. Her goal was also to train other pastors in the area for freedom ministry. By me training her and her training others, this was reaching people far and wide.

God continued to manifest this word throughout the day. Our teams went out to prophesy and pray over people in the mall. God had given me a word of knowledge earlier in my prayer time and told me what store to go to, where approximately I would find the person, and an hour time frame in which to do it. We arrived at the store, and my assistant felt led to go over to the same person I was looking for. When we evangelize we also give people a business card so that if they need follow-up care they know that they can call us for assistance or for us to direct them to the appropriate person or ministry. The lady we handed the card to ended up calling us within hours and confessing that she tried to kill herself the previous day.

During our time of mall evangelism we were also led to go into a shoe store. There was a young lady there who had been seeking a ministry similar to ours in which to volunteer. It was a divine connection, and we spent time talking, speaking with her, and showing her love. Both of these mall encounters were reaching people far and wide because when we reach people, equip them, and show them love it will have a domino effect throughout their lives.

We continued reaching people in the mall and also stopped by a jewelry store to show love to some ladies. A customer service representative came over to me. She ended up being a Christian, but we still showed her love. Of course, with me liking jewelry, I took a brief look while I was talking to her. We were in the clearance section, and a ruby ring stood out to me. When I asked her how much it was I couldn't believe how inexpensive it was. However, with the negotiating skills I have acquired, I still wanted to see what I could do to lower the price. God gave me divine favor and unexpected blessings, as I purchased a huge Chatham ruby ring with white sapphire baguettes in sterling silver for only fifty dollars. It was gorgeous, and I know the Spirit was leading me to purchase it. (He has a tendency to have me bless people with jewelry.)

I wonder what results my day would or would not have had if I had not spoken out my prayers. We have to speak out what the Lord is calling us to speak. However, laziness and tiredness keep us praying in our minds more than declaring out things in order to receive the blessings of God.

I don't believe God does all of this and that I have all of these testimonies as stories simply to bless me. I believe that when God blesses me, partially the reason He is doing it is to bless you! He wants you to see the fruit of your lips and the answers to your prayers. He desires for you to see the rewards of obedience and discipline in prayer. He wants to bless you too!

Come on, people of God; you can rain down blessing, change your situation, and manifest your healing by praying out loud and calling forth what He is leading you to pray. Think about what could happen if you sought Him each morning for direction on what to speak out, proclaim out, and declare out. What could change? Would your healing manifest or loved ones repent, change, and turn around and follow Jesus?

Daily we speak out and declare things out of our mouth without even realizing it. Simple sentences that are part of our everyday conversations can impart life:

It's a beautiful day out!

I'm blessed and highly favored!

I'm happy!

This is going to be a fantastic day!

Speaking out positive statements are life, and they call forth the good things in your day. However, there are also negative things we speak out daily that we are unaware of, statements such as:

- "I'm sick."
- "I feel irritated/frustrated."
- "I'm not feeling well today."
- "I'm not satisfied in my marriage, job, or life."
- "I'm not being fed spiritually in my church."
- "I don't have money for that."

Do you really want to claim that you are sick, or do you want to get up and fight the devil with the Word of God and kick that sickness and disease out of your body? Too often we fall into a victim mentality instead of a victorious attitude when physical afflictions hit our bodies. Jesus purchased our healing and deliverance two thousand years ago. We need to remember the victory has already been won. Speaking defeat about our church, finances, and marriage will only have us feeling weighed down and pessimistic.

When you speak these things often, do you feel edified? No, you leave the conversation reminded of your problems. We are not ignoring our problems; we simply want to state them differently as a declaration to claim the positive outcome of our problem. There is a time to state the facts of what is happening to us, but you need to ask yourself if you are speaking to someone who is going to stand by you in prayer with faith or assist you in getting the answer to your problem. If you are simply stating the facts in a conversation that is unproductive or unfruitful, you are much better off not even releasing those words into the spiritual atmosphere.

Words that go out in the atmosphere go somewhere. You want to be careful where your words are being assigned and released. You don't want to own your condition or situation by saying, "I have..." You want to speak it out as something that is manifesting in your body or as a spiritual attack upon your marriage, job, or family. You don't deny it; you're just not taking possession of it. Sometimes the way we speak about a situation takes possession where possession shouldn't be taken. It is not who you are; it is what is happening to you at the moment. To help renew your thinking and change the words you speak out of your mouth, here are some examples:

INSTEAD OF SAYING...	SAY INSTEAD...
"I have cancer."	*The doctor has diagnosed me with cancer, but I am taking my authority and claiming the Word that by Jesus stripes I am healed.*
"I have a headache."	*A headache is attacking my body.*
"I am pre-diabetic."	*I am watching my sugar intake and how it affects my body.*
"I have indigestion."	*My body is not reacting well to the food I ate.*

In Proverbs 18:21 it says, "Death and life are in the power of the tongue, And those who love it will eat its fruit" (Prov. 18:21). When we look at this verse it really is the law of sowing and reaping: "Do not be deceived, God is not mocked; for whatever a man sows, that he will also reap. For he who sows to his flesh will of the flesh reap corruption, but he who sows to the Spirit will of the Spirit reap everlasting life" (Gal. 6:7-8). We have been taught that we will reap what we sow in financial giving and servanthood. I also believe this to be true with our words. Too many people are in a victim mentality, speaking out negativity over their situation, and they do not see their circumstances change. People talk about their problems instead of speaking into the spiritual atmosphere. We must train ourselves to call forth the spirit realm to activate in a positive manner, stepping into their problem to create change.

Remember, "death and life are in the power of… [our] tongue" (Prov. 18:21)! Do you want to be speaking out negativity or positivity? The choice is yours, but I am here to tell you that, in the Bible, situations changed when people spoke to them. Fig trees withered (Matt. 21:19), blind eyes were opened (Mark 10:51), and Lazarus was raised from the dead (John 11:43)!

What are you establishing with your words? *Establish* means "to begin, build, implement, initiate, organize, originate, and start." When you speak, you are activating the spirit realm. It goes both ways. We can establish good or bad, but by focusing on the positive and watching our word choices carefully we can make sure we are establishing great and mighty things for our family and ministry. Your mouth and the words that come forth from it establish a positive or negative atmosphere.

We should constantly be thinking of what positive things we can speak out. When someone sneezes most people will respond with, "Bless you," or, "God bless you." When I say, "God bless you," I mean it! I know it will establish a blessing in their life! Instead of saying good-bye to a person, when I leave them I speak an establishment over them, such as, "May God grant you favor today," "Blessings to you," or, "Have a great day." I believe that what I speak over a person will happen. Our words are an establishment, a start, a beginning of something!

I was raised in a poverty mentality, and it took me years to see that I was putting some of that on my children by the words I spoke. I inadvertently trained my children at a young age how to speak about lack and not having the money to always purchase what they desired. I remember the countless shopping trips to the store or the conversations at home where they would want an item, and I would have to tell them that we can't afford it. Upon learning the power of my authority as a believer in Christ and that there are words we speak that are not profitable, I decided my family had to change the way we spoke. I made a choice to change my words, to speak life into our finances, and taught my children to do the same. Instead of saying, "We can't afford that," I would say, "I am choosing to spend my money elsewhere," or, "I am waiting for our financial blessing to manifest." My children learned to ask, "Mommy, when our financial blessing manifests, can I have this?" I taught my children to not speak negative words from their mouths. When we change our word choices we set in motion processes that can change our situation. I know that at least it will renew our mind. And, when it comes to finances we could all stand to increase our expectations and hope for the best.

There is power in our words because the Bible says, "Assuredly, I say to you, whatever you bind on earth will be bound in heaven, and whatever you loose on earth will be loosed in heaven" (Matt. 18:18). There is a correlation here. When we bind and loose, what happens in the natural will happen in the spiritual, and what happens in the spiritual will happen in the natural. When we study binding and loosing we discover that heaven agrees with what has happened because in heaven it has been accomplished, and heaven stands behind us!

> Yes! I tell you people that whatever you prohibit on earth will be prohibited in heaven,

and whatever you permit on earth will be
permitted in heaven.

—Matthew 18:18, cjb

Truly I tell you, whatever you forbid and
declare to be improper and unlawful on earth
must be what is already forbidden in heaven,
and whatever you permit and declare proper
and lawful on earth must be what is already
permitted in heaven.

—Matthew 18:18, ampc

It is similar to the fact that Jesus died on the cross
for us over two thousand years ago. He purchased our
salvation, healing, and deliverance. People are trying
to get something they already have. You simply need to
receive what Jesus already did: "But He was wounded for
our transgressions, He was bruised for our iniquities; The
chastisement for our peace was upon Him, And by His
stripes we are healed" (Isa. 53:5). We are healed, saved,
and delivered by what He already accomplished at the
cross. He has more blessings to give us that have already
been released in heaven. We need to believe, receive, and
command them to come down from heaven to Earth. In
the Lord's Prayer we are reminded again of the heaven
and Earth correlation: "Your kingdom come. Your will be
done On earth as it is in heaven" (Matt. 6:10).

God has things already established and completed for
us in heaven. When it has been set aside for us in heaven
and we don't see it yet on Earth, that's when we have
to call the things that don't exist yet into existence. We
have to live and believe as though they do exist: "In the
presence of Him whom he believed—God, who gives life

to the dead and calls those things which do not exist as though they did" (Rom. 4:17).

Jesus and the Father spoke to things. I will give further illustration of this in another chapter. Jesus and the Father verbally spoke, and things were created, objects responded, and people were healed: "For He spoke, and it was done; He commanded, and it stood fast" (Ps. 33:9). Speak to things and believe! Consider it done, as when Jesus said, "It is finished" (John 19:30). Command what you need to come into existence, and bind and restrict the demonic realm from working in your life. Stand fast and persevere while waiting for the manifestation. Don't give up, and don't allow doubt to come into your heart. Go back and read in the Bible all of the wonderful things that happened and believe they can happen for you too!

Jesus believed in the power of His words: "And seeing a fig tree by the road, He came to it and found nothing on it but leaves, and said to it, 'Let no fruit grow on you ever again.' Immediately the fig tree withered away" (Matt. 21:19). He spoke to this fig tree in front of people. He modeled how to speak to things. He believed the fig tree would wither away. You need to believe that the dead in your life that is supposed to stay dead will wither away. Stop trying to resurrect the dead in your life, bringing up problems you have already been healed of and have conquered. You are more than a conqueror through Christ Jesus!

When Jesus died, He gave us His power and authority: "Behold, I give you the authority to trample on serpents and scorpions, and over all the power of the enemy, and nothing shall by any means hurt you" (Luke 10:19). He transferred His power and authority to us as He ascended into heaven. It is similar to when a person on Earth gets the power of attorney over another person. Jesus left this earth and gave you the same authority as someone with the power of attorney to act in another person's name. You need to take that authority and speak to the conditions in your life that need to go and not return.

In order to speak to your condition, knowing who you are in Christ is important. You discover who you are in Christ by reading the Word of God and discovering that the very Word of God is talking about you. You find out who you are in Christ by discovering your kingdom inheritance and that you are a son or daughter of the most high King. As you establish who Christ is in your life and understand the connection you have with the Father, you will discover your true identity. When someone asks us who we are, our response should not be, "I am a doctor," "I am a pastor," or, "I am a cashier." Those identifications are your job description or career. You are not a divorcee, an alcoholic, or a cancer survivor. Don't allow the circumstances or trials you went through or conditions you were plagued with to identify you. Your answer should be, "I am a son or daughter of Jesus Christ, beloved and cherished by my heavenly Father." Your inheritance is that all of heaven responds when you call! Hallelujah! That is reason enough to speak out and celebrate. Heaven is waiting to respond to your request. Why don't you start speaking out right now?

Jesus said, "For assuredly, I say to you, whoever says to this mountain, 'Be removed and be cast into the sea,' and does not doubt in his heart, but believes that those things he says will be done, he will have whatever he says" (Mark 11:23). Speak out! Jesus instructed us to! He instructed us to speak, not to think about it, not to ponder it. He desired us to speak to our situation.

We have not been taught to speak to things, even though the Bible instructs us to. It seems foreign to pray out loud, to speak out loud, and to speak to things and possessions. The church hasn't taught us to speak to angels and demons and make them obey our words. However, we do see that Jesus spoke to demons, and they left. (See Mark 1:25; Luke 4:35.) They were quiet, and they departed the region. If we are supposed to be like Jesus, and I know we are, then we should be following the model He gave us while He was on Earth and speaking to our situations.

Since we are in a relationship with Jesus we have faith like Jesus had.

> And since we have the same spirit of faith, according to what is written, "I believed and therefore I spoke," we also believe and therefore speak.
> —2 Corinthians 4:13

When we speak we need to believe. But also, when we speak we hear what we have spoken, and that activates our belief system: "So then faith comes by hearing, and hearing by the word of God" (Rom. 10:17). Whether we hear a Scripture from the Word of God or a declaration that we have personally written or have been inspired by the Holy Spirit to write when we speak out, we hear it, and it increases our belief system.

Our words in the natural need to align with our faith in the spiritual. It will not benefit us if we are speaking words out of legalism and doubt. We cannot go into robot mode and speak things out without the belief system to line up with what we are speaking. There is a correlation between the natural and the spiritual, and our responsibility is to make sure that they connect within us. We make that connection by getting to know our heavenly Father better in order to grow our faith. By spending time in the Word of God and realizing that Word is for us, we will grow in our faith. As we connect with the Father through prayer and worship, we will build up our faith, and then "whatever things you ask in prayer, believing, you will receive" (Matt. 21:22).

When you align your prayers and declarations up to believing, you receive. It really is that plain and simple. We need to go back to the simplicity of the gospel and believe that it will accomplish what it says it will. As Christians we have overcomplicated the gospel, always having to analyze it and question if it is really for us. We ponder it and wonder if what it says is true or if it will happen. The gospel is truth! Believe it, and receive it for yourself! It is not only for everyone else; it is for you too!

Our Father desires us to live in the light (1 John 2:10) and the love of Christ, to have that same resurrection life of Christ flowing through us. Jesus came to set the captives free and give us a victorious life! He declared, "The Spirit of the Lord GOD is upon Me, Because the LORD has anointed Me To preach good tidings to the poor; He has sent Me to heal the brokenhearted, To proclaim liberty to the captives, And the opening of the prison to those who are bound" (Isa. 61:1; see Luke 4:17-21). The Father sent Jesus to come and model how to have a life of freedom. John 8:12 records that "Jesus spoke to them again, saying, 'I am the light of the world. He who follows Me shall not walk in darkness, but have the light of life.'" If we are to walk in the light, then we must take control over our situation and make sure we are binding and restricting the demonic realm over our lives and calling forth every good and perfect thing (James 1:17).

There is power in the out-spoken word when we ask according to God's will. He knows what His will is for our lives and what He desires to impart. We need to make sure when we are asking that what we are seeking from Him is to accomplish His will. Therefore, when you ask, make sure you are not asking amiss (James 4:3).

Ask in Jesus' name. Jesus asked, and we can see in the Scriptures that He commanded things. He was Jesus and didn't have to say, "I ask this in Jesus' name." However, when we ask of the Father, quote Scripture to bind and restrict the demonic realm, or call something forth that is not, we should end our statement of command with, "In Jesus' name." Our power and authority comes in the name of Jesus. Paul did this when he cast out a demon: "And this she did for many days. But Paul, greatly annoyed, turned and said to the spirit, 'I command you in the name of Jesus Christ to come out of her.' And he came out that very hour" (Acts 16:18).

> And in that day you will ask Me nothing. Most assuredly, I say to you, whatever you ask the Father in My name He will give you.
> —John 16:23

Even here Jesus is instructing us to ask the Father. Often people have the mentality that if God wants to give them something He can. If that is the case, then why does the Bible instruct us to ask for what we want, to speak to our mountain? There are many action words in the Bible. There are actions we sometimes have to take to produce the results we are seeking.

The Bible instructs us to be active in our faith and asking. Matthew 7:7 tells us, "Ask, and it will be given to you; seek, and you will find; knock, and it will be opened to you." *Ask* is an action word. It means "to make a request" or "to call for." *To ask* is also defined as "to tell someone in the form of a question that you want to be given something or that you want something to happen." If you want something to happen in your life, put your faith into action through the power of the words that you speak.

When we are declaring and asking for what we desire, it is not always for a material possession or commanding a demonic spirit to leave. Declaring can be for our spiritual growth or for the advancement of the kingdom of God. The Bible tells us that He will allow us to possess the land: "Ask of Me, and I will give You The nations for Your inheritance, And the ends of the earth for Your possession" (Ps. 2:8). By inquiring of Him to expand our territories, it can leave a door wide open to lift up the name of Jesus and spread His name far and wide. The ultimate desire should be to glorify the name of Jesus with the end results of whatever we receive through our declaration. The test of our heart and declaration should be, Will the end results glorify the Lord? Even Jesus was seeking in the last hour that the Father's name should be glorified. He did not glorify Himself but desired for the Father to be glorified.

> Jesus spoke these words, lifted up His eyes to heaven, and said: "Father; the hour has come. Glorify Your Son, that Your Son also may glorify You."
>
> —JOHN 17:1

I remember a couple of different times when I was declaring for things. The first one was for a building for our ministry. I had a businessman come in and make a wonderful offer. I prayed and sought the Father. I remember driving to the building to try and discern if it was for me. I would sing the song "Exalted" by Chris Tomlin on the way to the building. Those lyrics would hit me and remind me of Psalm 99:5: "Exalt the LORD our God, And worship at His footstool—He is holy." How I just desired to have His name exalted! I didn't end up getting the building. Even though it was a wonderful offer, it wasn't free. God promised me a free building. I desired His name to be fully exalted with the complete testimony, not partially with a payment I would have to make.

Another time, years later, God performed a miracle and provided for my son and I both to receive free cars within a couple of weeks of each other. We actually both received the money from different people within five days of each other. I remember driving down the street talking to my son. I said, "You know what I am so stoked about? That the name of Jesus Christ is going to be glorified." God told me that the testimony of these vehicles would go far and wide. To His name be the glory!

God desires to give us good gifts. Jesus reminded us, "If you then, being evil, know how to give good gifts to your children, how much more will your Father who is in heaven give good things to those who ask Him!" (Matt. 7:11). He desires for us to have the longing of our hearts. His Bible is one of prosperity! He doesn't desire us to live in lack but have the abundance of heaven poured out for us. When we are pure in heart and seek Him, and when glorifying His name is in our best interest, He will provide for us. We simply have to check ourselves continually and examine our motives for the blessing we want to receive.

Jesus asked when healing the blind man, "What do you want Me to do for you?" (Mark 10:36). Jesus wanted this man to speak out of his mouth into the spiritual atmosphere for his healing. Jesus was modeling the power of speaking out. This man's words aligned with his faith for healing. Jesus said, "According to your faith let it be [done] to you" (Matt. 9:29). If the man didn't speak, the healing might not have happened.

I do this in my ministry today when prompted by the Holy Spirit. I ask people, "If you had a silver platter in front of you, if God would give you anything, what would you ask for?" They speak it out, and God does the rest. I have never had one person speak out that they want the platter full of money. They are usually asking for spiritual things, and God loves to give spiritual things. Speak out! What do you want Jesus to do for you? Put your natural circumstance into a prophetic proclamation and believe for your situation to change.

I believe we can ask people what they want healing for, and I use this model for healing as the Spirit leads me. People can assume that Christian ministers know it all. There are ministers who have discernment and can tell what the person is coming up to receive in prayer. The Holy Spirit can also give the minister a word of knowledge. However, I believe Jesus modeled the power of our words. He asked the two blind men sitting on the side of the road what they wanted from Him. They were sitting on the side of the road and called out to Jesus: "So Jesus stood still and called them, and said, 'What do you want Me to do for you?' They said to Him, 'Lord, that our eyes may be opened.' So Jesus had compassion and touched their eyes. And immediately their eyes received sight, and they followed Him" (Matt. 20:32-34). Jesus had them declare out what they wanted, and it changed their situation.

All through the Bible it talks about the out-spoken word: to speak to our mountains, that death and life are in the power of the tongue, and to call things that are not as if they were. He made a particular man activate his words to receive his healing. What are we not receiving because we don't activate our words? We must learn the power of speaking out instead of being complacent. I believe there are many things that are not manifesting in our lives because we sit around waiting for something to happen instead of doing something to make it happen.

For years, whenever I would get a cold, I would succumb to it. I would tell people that I had a cold or the flu and was going to lie on the couch for three days and ride it out and rest. I was letting the sickness and disease penetrate my body and make me feel miserable. When you feel miserable you don't feel like praying, worshiping, and reading your Bible. These colds didn't just knock me on the floor physically; they took me out spiritually because I did nothing about them. After I learned my authority in Christ and the healing Jesus purchased for me on the cross I said, "No more!" When those infirmities try to attack me there is no more laying on the couch for me. I get on my war boots.

> And from the days of John the Baptist until now the kingdom of heaven suffers violence, and the violent take it by force.
> —MATTHEW 11:12

I get up and get violent in prayer. I claim, command, and decree for my body to come into alignment with the Word of God, which says by His stripes, I am healed!

> But He was wounded for our transgressions; He was bruised for our iniquities; The chastisement

for our peace was upon Him, And by His stripes we are healed.

—Isaiah 53:5

Who Himself bore our sins in His own body on the tree, that we, having died to sins, might live for righteousness—by whose stripes you were healed.

—1 Peter 2:24

I speak to that sickness and disease out loud, commanding it to leave my body and for my body to be healed in Jesus' name. I say, "Cold, infirmity, get out of me! Stuffy nose, clear up! Headache, be gone, in Jesus' name." I don't put up with it. I get holy, righteous anger. I take my authority and know that sickness and disease cannot exist inside my body. In the last several years I have not had a cold or flu manifest more than ten percent of the time. When it rises up I take my vitamin C, speak to my condition, and claim the Word of God over my body. It has to obey my instructions to leave.

There was another time when I saw the power of my words manifest. I went to Georgia to do a healing crusade and met a person that I wanted to be involved with through ministry. I could tell that he was a holy and humble man of God. I left that event, and for months each time I talked about the event or the man I would speak out of my mouth, "I will have that man for my spiritual father." I didn't hear from him except for about three times after that, but I kept declaring it. He had something I wanted, an authentic heart of the Father and a deep relationship with Him. He also had great wisdom. I kept declaring it by faith. He called me up a few months later and asked me to do a conference with him, an invitation I prayerfully

45

accepted. We met a few months before the conference and further got to discover each other's love for the Lord.

I went home and continued to declare out that I would have him for my spiritual father. I did not pray and petition and spend hours upon hours in prayer. I made simple statements into the spiritual atmosphere with faith to believe that I would receive. God was revealing that something would happen the weekend I was with him for the conference, but I did not know exactly what it was, except that he and I together would work on breaking down the walls of racism.

Before the conference we sat together for a meeting. During that time, he asked me, "What do you want? What have you been asking of God?" I said, "There is only one thing I want of you and that I have been declaring out of my mouth, that you would be my spiritual father." He said, "I receive you and your ministry." He knew. My spiritual father had heard from the heavenly Father what I was inquiring of him. This man was in communication with the Father, and he told me what I had been declaring.

God knows what you want, but you have to ask for it. The Father wants you to ask for it. I had to take that prophetic action and speak it out, just as Jesus made the blind man do. It is biblical to decree, speak out, and ask. The Father knows this and has confirmed it so many times. I hope and pray that you receive this revelation of how powerful the concept of declaring is.

I remember being on the plane flying to Georgia thinking, "Will I ask him? How will this happen? Will it happen this time?" All of these thoughts and what if's were running through my mind, but they didn't need to. My heavenly Father had already heard the plea of my heart and the declaration of my mouth. He knew I had the faith to believe and receive it. My Father went ahead of me and prepared my heart and put my words in alignment with my faith for it. I spoke it! I received it! My heavenly Father also went before me and prepared this man's heart to be my overseer. He knew what I wanted, what I desired. He was so close to the Father that the Father revealed what I had been declaring to Him. But, still, the Father wanted me to speak it out.

The Father will go before you too and prepare the way. He will grant the desires and petitions of your heart in accordance with His will. The question is, Will you, can you, take the step of faith to speak it out and believe for it? Do you believe there is power in the words you speak out? Do you have the faith to believe, to decree, to receive? There is no partiality with God. What He did for me, He can do for you!

Words had power in the story of David and Goliath.

> Then he stood and cried out to the armies of Israel, and said to them, "Why have you come out to line up for battle? Am I not a Philistine, and you the servants of Saul? Choose a man for yourselves, and let him come down to me."
>
> —1 Samuel 17:8

Goliath was trying to win the battle with his words. He cried out—verbally, out loud—in threats. He made himself sound superior, and the Israelites believed it and were afraid.

Goliath was relentless and went day and night to intimidate the Israelites with his words. We could learn from Goliath. Often we declare or pray for a particular circumstance, and we consider it done and finished. Sometimes that is the case. But there are also times when we need to be relentless and continually declare out, speak out, what we are hoping for.

The battlefield is in our mind. We pray and declare but can also doubt at the same time. As we speak out and declare we will conquer the battle in our mind. There is something about faith arising when we decree out loud. We can feel invigorated and strong, powerful and authoritative. Speak out your prayer declarations and see what results you can produce.

On the way to win the battle David went in unprotected in the natural but more than protected in the spiritual.

> So Saul clothed David with his armor, and he put a bronze helmet on his head; he also clothed him with a coat of mail. David fastened his sword to his armor and tried to walk, for he had not tested them. And David said to Saul, "I cannot walk with these, for I have not tested them." So David took them off. Then he took his staff in his hand; and he chose for himself five smooth stones from the brook, and put them in a shepherd's bag, in a pouch which he had, and his sling was in his hand. And he drew near to the Philistine.
>
> —1 Samuel 17:38-40

When declaring, we can build up our spiritual faith by putting on the armor of God, studying the Word of God, and praying. These are natural things we can do that have spiritual results. When we build ourselves up in the spirit in faith, then the manifestation of what we are believing for will become reality. We need faith and persistence to call forth our blessings.

So the Philistine came, and began drawing near to David, and the man who bore the shield went before him. And when the Philistine looked about and saw David, he disdained him; for he was only a youth, ruddy and good-looking.

—1 SAMUEL 17:41-42

David declared out and prophesied over himself the victory he would have. He spoke out, decreed, and declared what he was expecting.

Then David said to the Philistine, "You come to me with a sword, with a spear, and with a javelin. But I come to you in the name of the LORD of hosts, the God of the armies of Israel, whom you have defied. This day the LORD will deliver you into my hand, and I will strike you and take your head from you. And this day I will give the carcasses of the camp of the Philistines to the birds of the air and the wild beasts of the earth, that all the earth may know that there is a God in Israel. Then all this assembly shall know that the LORD does not save with sword and spear; for the battle is the LORD's, and He will give you into our hands."

—1 SAMUEL 17:45-47

David went in the name of his Lord. We too need to declare and go forth in the name of our Lord. We need David's confidence and boldness that as we go forward God will perform His Word and promises to us. David had to go forth in word and action. Even though some of us will not have to take a physical action, we need to go forward in the same confidence through the words we speak.

David prophesied in advance what was going to happen. That is a valuable example for us. There is power in our words, and we can prophesy in advance over ourselves the victory that is going to happen in our lives. The Bible says to speak to your mountain, that there is power in our outspoken words, and that death and life are in the power of the tongue. We need to prophesy out of our mouths the victory that we want to come to pass. It also could be closely compared to claiming, commanding, and decreeing.

> So it was, when the Philistine arose and came and drew near to meet David, that David hurried and ran toward the army to meet the Philistine. Then David put his hand in his bag and took out a stone; and he slung it and struck the Philistine in his forehead, so that the stone sank into his forehead, and he fell on his face to the earth. So David prevailed over the Philistine with a sling and a stone, and struck the Philistine and killed him. But there was no sword in the hand of David. Therefore David ran and stood over the Philistine, took his sword and drew it out of its sheath and killed him, and cut off his head with it. And when the Philistines saw that their champion was dead, they fled.
>
> —1 SAMUEL 17:48-51

David was victorious. David believed what would come forth and received it. He had assurance, faith, and trust. And when declaring we need those same things. We need to acknowledge like David did that our battle is the Lord's battle. When we are speaking out and declaring we are doing the Lord's bidding.

David was eager to fight and prepared for the battle in his heart. He embraced his assignment. We too need to be prepared for whatever assignment the Spirit has called us to declare. David had confidence. He had no fear or intimidation. He had boldness, and in Hebrews it says that we may come boldly before the throne (Heb. 4:16).

I believe that what we receive or don't receive is sometimes contingent on our approach. Are we believing for what we will receive? Are we being diligent to repeatedly declare out and prophesy over ourselves what we are expecting or are called to pray for? David went forward; he didn't look to the left or the right but stayed on the course and had victory. Likewise, we need to keep looking forward and declaring for the prosperity and revelation of heaven as a manifestation of the promises of God that we long to see for ourselves.

Words can have a negative influence on us also. What we speak out can come back and influence us in a manner that we don't want to experience.

> But I say to you that for every idle word men may speak, they will give account of it in the day of judgment. For by your words you will be justified, and by your words you will be condemned
>
> —MATTHEW 12:36-37

In Genesis 27 we see how Rebekah's words brought upon her and her family a curse that followed them for years to come:

> Now it came to pass when Isaac was old and his eyes were so dim that he could not see, that he called Esau his older son and said to him, "My

son." And he answered him, "Here I am." Then he said, "Behold now, I am old. I do not know the day of my death. Now therefore, please take your weapons, your quiver and your bow, and go out to the field and hunt game for me. And make me savory food, such as I love, and bring it to me that I may eat, that my soul may bless you before I die." Now Rebekah was listening when Isaac spoke to Esau his son. And Esau went to the field to hunt game and to bring it. So Rebekah spoke to Jacob her son, saying, "Indeed I heard your father speak to Esau your brother, saying, 'Bring me game and make savory food for me, that I may eat it and bless you in the presence of the LORD before my death.' Now therefore, my son, obey my voice according to what I command you. Go now to the flock and bring me from there two choice kids of the goats, and I will make savory food from them for your father, such as he loves. Then you shall take it to your father, that he may eat it, and that he may bless you before his death." And Jacob said to Rebekah his mother, "Look, Esau my brother is a hairy man, and I am a smooth-skinned man. Perhaps my father will feel me, and I shall seem to be a deceiver to him; and I shall bring a curse on myself and not a blessing." But his mother said to him, "Let your curse be on me, my son; only obey my voice, and go, get them for me." And he went and got them and brought them to his mother, and his mother made savory food, such as his father loved. Then Rebekah took the choice clothes of her elder son Esau, which were with her in the house, and put them on Jacob her younger son. And she put the skins of the kids of the goats on his hands and on the smooth part of his neck. Then she gave the savory food and the bread, which she had prepared, into the hand of her son Jacob. So he went to his father and said, "My father." And he said, "Here I am. Who are you, my son?" Jacob said to his father, "I am Esau your firstborn; I have done just as you told me; please arise, sit and eat of my game, that your soul may bless me." But Isaac said to his son, "How is it that you have found it so quickly, my son?" And he said, "Because the LORD your God brought it to me." Isaac said to Jacob, "Please come near, that I may feel you, my son, whether you are really my son Esau or not." So Jacob went near to Isaac his father, and he felt him and said, "The voice is Jacob's voice, but the hands are the hands of Esau." And he did not recognize him, because his hands were hairy like his brother Esau's hands; so he blessed him. Then he said, "Are you really my son Esau?" He said, "I am." He said, "Bring it near to me, and I will eat of my son's game, so that my soul may bless you." So he brought it near to him, and he ate; and he brought him wine, and he drank. Then his father Isaac said to him, "Come near now and kiss me, my son." And he came near and kissed him; and he smelled the smell of his clothing, and blessed him and said: "Surely, the smell of my son Is like the smell of a field Which the LORD has blessed. Therefore may God give you Of the dew of heaven, Of the fatness of the earth, And plenty of grain and wine. Let peoples serve you, And nations bow down to you. Be master over your brethren, And let your mother's sons bow down to you. Cursed be everyone who curses you, And blessed be those who bless you!" Now it happened, as soon as Isaac had finished blessing Jacob, and Jacob had scarcely gone out from the presence of Isaac his father, that Esau his brother came in from his hunting. He also had made savory food, and brought it to his father, and said to his father, "Let my father arise and eat of his son's game, that your soul may bless me." And his father Isaac said to him, "Who are you?" So he said, "I am your son, your firstborn, Esau." Then Isaac trembled exceedingly, and said, "Who? Where is the one who hunted game and brought it to me? I ate all of it before you came, and I have blessed him— and indeed he shall be blessed." When Esau heard the words of his father, he cried with an exceedingly great and bitter cry, and said to his father, "Bless me—me also, O my father!" But he said, "Your brother came with deceit and has taken away your blessing." And Esau said, "Is he not rightly named Jacob? For he has supplanted me these two times. He took away my birthright, and now look, he has taken away my blessing!" And he said, "Have you not reserved a blessing for me?" Then Isaac answered and said to Esau, "Indeed I have made him your master, and all his brethren I have given to him as servants; with grain and wine I have sustained him. What shall I do now for you, my son?" And Esau said to his father, "Have you only one blessing, my father? Bless me—me also, O my father!" And Esau lifted up his voice and wept. Then Isaac his father answered and said to him: "Behold, your dwelling shall be of the fatness of the earth, And of the dew of heaven from above. By your sword you shall live, And you shall serve your brother; And it shall come to pass, when you become restless, That you shall break his yoke from your neck." So Esau hated Jacob because of the blessing with which his father blessed him, and Esau said in his heart, "The days of mourning for my father are at hand; then I will kill my brother Jacob." And the words of Esau her older son were told to Rebekah. So she sent and called Jacob her younger son, and said to him, "Surely your brother Esau comforts himself concerning you by intending to kill you. Now therefore, my son, obey my voice: arise, flee to my brother Laban in Haran. And stay with him a few days, until your brother's fury turns away, until your brother's anger turns away from you, and he forgets what you have done to him; then I will send and bring you from there. Why should I be bereaved also of you both in one day?" And Rebekah said to Isaac, "I am weary of my life because of the daughters of Heth; if Jacob takes a wife of the daughters of Heth, like these who are the daughters of the land, what good will my life be to me?"

—GENESIS 27

Rebekah was persuading her son Jacob to deceive Isaac, his father, now blind, in order to obtain his blessing, a blessing which Isaac intended to pronounce on his other son, Esau. Jacob was eager for the blessing but fearful of the consequences if Isaac should discover his deception. "Perhaps my father will feel me," he said, "and I shall seem to be a deceiver to him; and I shall bring a curse on myself and not a blessing" (v. 12). Rebekah responded immediately,

"Let your curse be on me, my son" (v. 13). And the curse was on Rebekah, and she lost the privilege of being with her son. This is the power of your words in action!

Self-invited word curses can affect you and those around you. I know a person who used to speak out, "I have a love-hate relationship with my sister. Half of the time we love each other, and half of the time it is a challenge being around her." This is a word curse. Similar to Rebekah, she was speaking out with her words a self-invited curse. However, this was also a generational curse. Her parents both had this kind of relationship with their siblings, except much worse, where they wouldn't talk to their siblings for years. She had taken what started out as a generational curse and made it her own. She took ownership of the words and situation and applied it to her circumstances through her words. Her situation was not going to improve if she kept speaking out those words, because, as we see with Rebekah, there is power in our words.

Familiar spirits and generational spirits target our families and situations that are familiar to us. These spirits have been assigned to our genealogy and know our families' past mistakes and weaknesses. We also need to be aware of the word curses and generational curses in our family members' lives so that we don't repeat the past and bring what is dead, buried, and gone into the future. We need to make sure that we are speaking life and freedom and not cursing and bondage. By the words we speak we can replant and build what the enemy has stolen of our past.

When Jesus was crucified we see another case of a curse. The curse was not only upon the people involved at that time but on the generational line of those affected by it;

ever since the words were spoken that curse continued itself throughout future generations.

> But the chief priests and elders persuaded the multitudes that they should ask for Barabbas and destroy Jesus. The governor answered and said to them, "Which of the two do you want me to release to you?" They said, "Barabbas!" Pilate said to them, "What then shall I do with Jesus who is called Christ?" They all said to him, "Let Him be crucified!" Then the governor said, "Why, what evil has He done?" But they cried out all the more, saying, "Let Him be crucified!" When Pilate saw that he could not prevail at all, but rather that a tumult was rising, he took water and washed his hands before the multitude, saying, "I am innocent of the blood of this just Person. You see to it." And all the people answered and said, "His blood be on us and on our children." Then he released Barabbas to them; and when he had scourged Jesus, he delivered Him to be crucified. Then the soldiers of the governor took Jesus into the Praetorium and gathered the whole garrison around Him. And they stripped Him and put a scarlet robe on Him. When they had twisted a crown of thorns, they put it on His head, and a reed in His right hand. And they bowed the knee before Him and mocked Him, saying, "Hail, King of the Jews!"
>
> —MATTHEW 27:20-29

Against his own judgment the Roman governor, Pilate, consented to release to the crowd a murderer named Barabbas and to impose the death sentence on Jesus instead. To disassociate himself from this act, however, Pilate washed his hands in front of the crowd and said, "I am innocent of the blood of this just Person" (v. 24). To this the crowd responded, "His blood be on us and on our children" (v. 25). Here there is a self-imposed curse on them and a relational curse on their descendants. Since that time bloodshed and tragedy have been entangled in the destiny of the Jewish people.

What self-imposed curses are you putting on yourself? What generational curses are you putting on your children? Statements such as the following should not be spoken:

- "She can't read."

- "She sings off key."

- "He always drops something."

- "My kids are loud and obnoxious."

- "Her middle name is Troublemaker."

Don't curse your children and spouse with your words. If it doesn't edify, encourage, or exhort, don't say it. Find a way to speak about a condition or happening that is not going to speak against anyone. Better yet, don't speak it at all if you aren't trying to find a solution to the problem.

How many times, like Rebekah, do we speak over ourselves and aren't even aware of it?

- Never say, "That makes me sick," when someone tells you something. It can open a doorway to sickness. You are speaking or claiming that something makes you sick! Think about it!

- Never say, "She's driving me crazy," or, "I can't take it anymore." Such statements can lead to emotional doors being opened. Do you really want to lose your mind and go crazy? How many times have you spoken that out over the years? Remember the law of sowing and reaping.

- Never say, "My daughter has the flu, and I'll catch it next." We are redeemed! We don't have to get the flu or a virus. Don't claim that it's going to attack you. Expectation is the breeding ground for miracles. Expect not to get sick; don't expect to get sick!

- Never say, "I can't afford to tithe!" Change your poverty mentality; you can't afford not to tithe.

- Never say, "Over my dead body," "I'm going to kill you for that," or, "You're going to kill me for this." Such statements open a door for spirits of death to come in.

- Never say, "They irritate me." That statement leads to a spirit of irritation. When you say that you are irritated or frustrated you can't get rid of it in a few days because you opened the door to those spirits by speaking it. Now you need to cast out a spirit of irritation or frustration. Listen to the words that you repeatedly say within a week.

The other challenge we have is that we've all been raised with comments by our parents, such as:

- "Be careful when driving so you don't get in an accident."

- "Watch out. The roads are going to be icy or slippery today."

- "You better not go near that person. They are sick, and you might catch it too."

We have been filled with concerns that create negativity in our minds. Worrisome parents think they are doing good when warning us what to do and not to do. The problem is that it causes us to have negative thoughts and worry. When those thoughts are spoken into our lives we can take them in and have them become who we are and what we speak. When we have those negative words spoken to us all of our lives, how can we not out of habit speak the same things to our children? As we grow up it only becomes natural that we speak out what has been spoken to us. Therefore, our word choices aren't the best. Since death and life are in our words, we have now spoken negatively over our children.

I remember several years ago as my children were starting to drive I had to hold my tongue back so many times. I knew I did not want to speak negative words as they left the house that could put them in fear and worry instead of joy and happiness about where they were going and what they were going to do.

Instead of saying, "Good-bye. Be blessed and highly favored, and have a great time tonight," and speaking life into them, we speak worry and negativity. When your children are going out the door, avoid saying, "Drive careful," "Watch out for deer or animals running out in front of you," "Be careful; it will be getting dark and rainy," or, "Make sure the kids in the car aren't goofing off and distracting you." Why not say a blessing over them? Turn the negative words you used to speak into positive declarations over your children. Speak to them as they leave with: "Good-bye. Have a good time. I love you. May the blood of Jesus cover you." "Love you, honey. I dispatch angels to guard and protect you tonight." Or, "Have a great time. The Lord, our God, goes with you and before you, and no weapon formed against you shall prosper."

By taking a few scriptures and incorporating them into the natural things you say when your child leaves your home, you can build their faith and teach the power of the out-spoken word. Our words are impactful, and we have choices to make every day. Be slow to speak and quick to discern and pay attention when the Holy Spirit says, "Don't speak that," because He will.

3
GOD SPOKE
AND CREATED

G OD SPOKE THE world into existence. It was the out-spoken words of His lips that created what we live in today. He spoke, and it was created. And since He made us in His image we can speak and see things created in our lives.

Then God said, "Let there be light"; and there was light. And God saw the light, that it was good; and God divided the light from the darkness. God called the light Day, and the darkness He called Night. So the evening and the morning were the first day. Then God said, "Let there be a firmament in the midst of the waters, and let it divide the waters from the waters." Thus God made the firmament, and divided the waters which were under the firmament from the waters which were above the firmament, and it was so. And God called the firmament Heaven. So the evening and the morning were the second day. Then God said, "Let the waters under the heavens be gathered together into one place, and let the dry land appear"; and it was so. And God called the dry land Earth, and the gathering together of the waters He called Seas. And God saw that it was good. Then God said, "Let the earth bring forth grass, the herb that yields seed, and the fruit tree that yields fruit according to its kind, whose seed is in itself, on the earth"; and it was so. And the earth brought forth grass, the herb that yields seed according to its kind, and the tree that yields fruit, whose seed is in itself according to its kind. And God saw that it was good. So the evening and the morning were the third day. Then God said, "Let there be lights in the firmament of the heavens to divide the day from the night; and let them be for signs and seasons, and for days and years; and let them be for lights in the firmament of the heavens to give light on the earth"; and it was so. Then God made two great lights: the greater light to rule the day, and the lesser light to rule the night. He made the stars also. God set them in the firmament of the heavens to give light on the earth, and to rule over the day and over the night, and to divide the light from the darkness. And God saw that it was good. So the evening and the morning were the fourth day. Then God said, "Let the waters abound with an abundance of living creatures, and let birds fly above the earth across the face of the firmament of the heavens." So God created great sea creatures and every living thing that moves, with which the waters abounded, according to their kind, and every winged bird according to its kind. And God saw that it was good. And God blessed them, saying, "Be fruitful and multiply, and fill the waters in the seas, and let birds multiply on the earth." So the evening and the morning were the fifth day. Then God said, "Let the earth bring forth the living creature according to its kind: cattle and creeping thing and beast of the earth, each according to its kind"; and it was so. And God made the beast of the earth according to its kind, cattle according to its kind, and everything that creeps on the earth according to its kind. And God saw that it was good. Then God said, "Let Us make man in Our image, according to Our likeness; let them have dominion over the fish of the sea, over the birds of the air, and over the cattle, over all the earth and over every creeping thing that creeps on the earth." So God created man in His own image; in the image of God He created him; male and female He created them. Then God blessed them, and God said to them, "Be fruitful and multiply; fill the earth and subdue it; have dominion over the fish of the sea, over the birds of the air, and over every living thing that moves on the earth." And God said, "See, I have given you every herb that yields seed which is on the face of all the earth, and every tree whose fruit yields seed; to you it shall be for food. Also, to every beast of the earth, to every bird of the air, and to everything that creeps on the earth, in which there is life, I have given every green herb for food"; and it was so. Then God saw everything that He had made, and indeed it was very good. So the evening and the morning were the sixth day.

—GENESIS 1:3-31

God created and said it was good. He created life, plants, food, day, night, and more. He was pleased with what He created, and He did it by His words. If you notice, in Genesis 1 it repeatedly says, "And God said..." He didn't think, meditate, or ponder; He spoke.

We need to learn the difference between thinking, meditating, pondering, and praying. I believe that often we think and believe we are praying when actually we get caught up in pondering and thinking, which is not prayer. Prayer is petitioning the Father for the outcome of a situation and believing for the miraculous to manifest. Prayer is not casually pondering and thinking about the different scenarios that may occur. Prayer is taking action and speaking to the Father or the situation.

God wanted Moses to take action by speaking to the rock to produce water.

> Then the children of Israel, the whole congregation, came into the Wilderness of Zin in the first month, and the people stayed in Kadesh; and Miriam died there and was buried there. Now there was no water for the congregation; so they gathered together against Moses and Aaron. And the people contended with Moses and spoke, saying: "If only we had died when our brethren died before the LORD! Why have you brought up the assembly of the LORD into this wilderness, that we and our animals should die here? And why have you made us come up out of Egypt, to bring us to this evil place? It is not a place of grain or figs or vines or pomegranates; nor is there any water to drink." So Moses and Aaron went from the presence of the assembly to the door

of the tabernacle of meeting, and they fell on their faces. And the glory of the LORD appeared to them. Then the LORD spoke to Moses, saying, "Take the rod; you and your brother Aaron gather the congregation together. Speak to the rock before their eyes, and it will yield its water; thus you shall bring water for them out of the rock, and give drink to the congregation and their animals." So Moses took the rod from before the LORD as He commanded him. And Moses and Aaron gathered the assembly together before the rock; and he said to them, "Hear now, you rebels! Must we bring water for you out of this rock?" Then Moses lifted his hand and struck the rock twice with his rod; and water came out abundantly, and the congregation and their animals drank. Then the LORD spoke to Moses and Aaron, "Because you did not believe Me, to hallow Me in the eyes of the children of Israel, therefore you shall not bring this assembly into the land which I have given them." This was the water of Meribah, because the children of Israel contended with the LORD, and He was hallowed among them. Now Moses sent messengers from Kadesh to the king of Edom. "Thus says your brother Israel: 'You know all the hardship that has befallen us, how our fathers went down to Egypt, and we dwelt in Egypt a long time, and the Egyptians afflicted us and our fathers. When we cried out to the LORD, He heard our voice and sent the Angel and brought us up out of Egypt; now here we are in Kadesh, a city on the edge of your border. Please let us pass through your country. We will not pass through fields or vineyards, nor will we drink water from wells;

we will go along the King's Highway; we will not turn aside to the right hand or to the left until we have passed through your territory.' "Then Edom said to him, "You shall not pass through my land, lest I come out against you with the sword." So the children of Israel said to him, "We will go by the Highway, and if I or my livestock drink any of your water, then I will pay for it; let me only pass through on foot, nothing more." Then he said, "You shall not pass through." So Edom came out against them with many men and with a strong hand. Thus Edom refused to give Israel passage through his territory; so Israel turned away from him. Now the children of Israel, the whole congregation, journeyed from Kadesh and came to Mount Hor. And the LORD spoke to Moses and Aaron in Mount Hor by the border of the land of Edom, saying: "Aaron shall be gathered to his people, for he shall not enter the land which I have given to the children of Israel, because you rebelled against My word at the water of Meribah. Take Aaron and Eleazar his son, and bring them up to Mount Hor; and strip Aaron of his garments and put them on Eleazar his son; for Aaron shall be gathered to his people and die there." Moses did just as the LORD commanded, and they went up to Mount Hor in the sight of all the congregation. Moses stripped Aaron of his garments and put them on Eleazar his son; and Aaron died there on the top of the mountain. Then Moses and Eleazar came down from the mountain. Now when all the congregation saw that Aaron was dead, all the house of Israel mourned for Aaron thirty days.

—Numbers 20

God asked Moses to speak to the rock so that it would produce water for the people. Moses was angry and instead hit the rock twice. Moses did not declare out the power of his words as God told him to. Moses' being disobedient to speak to the rock when God told him to speak cost him the Promised Land. Can you imagine all that Moses saw— the Red Sea parting and the plagues being distributed? Then, nearing the end, he allowed his flesh to rise up and was disobedient to God. It caused him to forfeit the very thing that he had worked years to see delivered.

I believe there is a parallel to this story and us. How many of you believe you can speak to a rock and have it produce water or speak to a dishwasher and have the motor start running right or speak to an automobile and have it start working properly? We cannot choose which orders and instructions to act on obediently and which ones to act out in our flesh, doing things our own way. Our own way gets us in trouble; our flesh is unproductive. The Word tells us, "So then, those who are in the flesh cannot please God" (Rom. 8:8).

When our God spoke, things responded. It was accomplished! He spoke, and it was done. Things activated on His out-spoken word.

For He spoke, and it was done; He commanded, and it stood fast.

—Psalm 33:9

69

> He spoke, and there came swarms of flies, And
> lice in all their territory.
> —Psalm 105:31

> He spoke, and locusts came, Young locusts without
> number.
> —Psalm 105:34

Our Father God declared over Jesus, His Son. When we look at the story of Jesus being baptized in water and prophetically declared over we see that a series of events took place. Prophetic declarations will bring forth both results and warfare, but there is a positive aspect in knowing how to declare. When you know how to declare you can decree against the warfare that will attempt to attack your situation.

The Father spoke a prophetic declaration over His Son:

> And immediately, coming up from the water,
> He saw the heavens parting and the Spirit
> descending upon Him like a dove. Then a voice
> came from heaven, "You are My beloved Son, in
> whom I am well pleased."
> —Mark 1:10-11

God declared out loud! It was a declaration from our Father over His Son. As powerful as it was, immediately the devil came in and tried to test and tempt Jesus.

When we pray or think in our mind the devil and demons can't hear those thoughts. As we declare or a prophetic word is released, the out-spoken word is released into the atmosphere. Angels and demons are waiting right there to activate on the out-spoken word.

In Mark 1:12, we see that Jesus, after being baptized and filled with the Spirit, was led into the wilderness, where His temptation began.

> Immediately the Spirit drove Him into the wilderness. And He was there in the wilderness forty days, tempted by Satan, and was with the wild beasts; and the angels ministered to Him.
>
> —Mark 1:12-13

The first thing that happened after the prophetic proclamation was that the Spirit drove Jesus into the wilderness. After you make a prophetic declaration the Holy Spirit could also convict and direct you. He can give you instructions, such as to pray more, fast, worship, or read a particular passage in the Bible. God might tell you to go somewhere, do something, or speak to someone. The instructions can be very important to see the manifestation of what you desire.

God is the One who does what we need to be done. Through His Spirit He can drop an idea in a person's spirit, or He can convict someone to carry out His instructions. However, most of the time when something is carried out it has to be done by a person. That is why it is crucial to follow the Holy Spirit's instructions and do what He wants when He wants it done. You may need to be in the right place at the right time to make a natural connection or spiritual appointment. If you are disobedient or just don't feel like doing what He is asking then you could miss the divine blessing He has orchestrated for you.

At Jesus' baptism the declaration went forth, and then the spiritual battle began. This isn't so different from what we experience in our daily life. You are given a prophetic word, and once that word is spoken out into the atmosphere the devil and his demons just heard your destiny, blessing, or the plans God has for you. You can bet that he is going to try to do everything in his power to steal, kill, and destroy (John 10:10). It is during that time that you have to put on your game face, as my friend Greg would say. You have to get to war and fight the battle with the words of your mouth through prayer and firing all of the Scripture you can at the enemy and his plans against you.

Why do you think people don't see the manifestation of their prophetic words? Because they don't know how to war, fight, and declare through prayer against the spiritual battle that comes following those prophetic words. People give up waiting for their prophetic words to come. Meanwhile, they also get mad at God, believing that He withheld from them. It can lead to distrusting God, opening the door to doubt and unbelief instead of faith.

The battle begins when the declaration, whether prophetic or not, has been spoken. Therefore, the information in this book is crucial to assist us in not only releasing our prayers but in calling forth and establishing our prophetic destinies. By the teaching of the Scriptures, empowerment of the Spirit, and the releasing of declarations, destinies can be established, ministries launched, and a dark and hurting world can be brought into the love and light of Jesus Christ.

Satan tempted Jesus. He tested and tried Him, and he tests and tries us. Jesus stood His ground and declared out the written Word of God. Each time the devil came to Jesus He would quote Scriptures back. However, He made them a declaration and stood strong in His faith. We too need to stand on the Word of God and declare out Scriptures.

We can only declare out what we know. You can't put out what you haven't taken in. Reading the Bible, studying, and memorizing are important parts of our daily spiritual life. It would be nice to get a supernatural impartation of Scripture, but in reality that doesn't often happen. When studying my Bible, sometimes I am on the floor and I get tired and lay my head on my Bible. It would be great if during those times it would just soak into my brain and be imparted, but that doesn't happen. I have to pick up my Bible, study it, read it, and go back to it again and reread it in order to absorb and retain the Scriptures. You need to co-labor with the Holy Spirit. He will assist you in praying out the Scriptures, but you need to have an arsenal of memorized Scripture from which the Holy Spirit can draw and bring the remembrance to your spirit. I encourage you to build up that arsenal and get in the Scriptures. The number one thing I hear Christians say is that they don't read or understand their Bible. Study it as you would for a college exam. Cross-reference your version with other Bible versions to bring out the understanding, reading the footnotes and cross-referencing the related Scriptures that are in your margins.

Jesus went through a wilderness experience. As you are learning a different way to pray, decree, and declare, you may also feel like you are all alone. You may feel differently. People may be apprehensive, but buy them a book and perhaps you will gain a friend who understands declaring like you do. I always say, "You've prayed and you haven't seen the manifestation of all of your prayers, so what is it going to hurt to try something different?" When you can point your friends to the Scriptures and where Jesus and the Father declared, then your friends will turn skepticism into optimism.

Jesus fasted in the wilderness. His time of growing spiritually and being tested was filled with prayer and fasting. It is often in my times of prayer and fasting that the Holy Spirit will write declarations for me. He will put in my spirit what He wants me to write down and declare out. Powerful things happen when you go away and spend solitary time with the Father in order to receive instruction through the Spirit.

The prophetic declaration was spoken over Jesus, and He was tested and tried in the wilderness. Then His ministry launched! The first thing Jesus did when He came out of that experience was to cast out demons!

> Now there was a man in their synagogue with an unclean spirit. And he cried out, saying, "Let us alone! What have we to do with You, Jesus of Nazareth? Did You come to destroy us? I know who You are—the Holy One of God!" But Jesus rebuked him, saying, "Be quiet, and come out of him!" And when the unclean spirit had convulsed him and cried out with a loud voice, he came out of him.
>
> —MARK 1:23-26

The testing and declaration led Him into His destiny! So often we want the destiny without the ugly stuff that comes before our release. We have to embrace the process, because when we do we are refined and able to handle whatever comes next. God knows what is best for us. Often we release a declaration and think it is immediately going to come to pass. But there are things we need to experience and knowledge we need to gain while going through whatever God calls you to go through on the way to your blessing. Embrace the process, because when you do it will go quicker and easier!

Jesus continued His ministry after the Father's declaration by healing many of the sick:

> But Simon's wife's mother lay sick with a fever, and they told Him about her at once. So He came and took her by the hand and lifted her up, and immediately the fever left her. And she served them. At evening, when the sun had set, they brought to Him all who were sick and those who were demon-possessed. And the whole city was gathered together at the door. Then He healed many who were sick with various diseases, and cast out many demons; and He did not allow the demons to speak because they knew Him. Now in the morning, having risen a long while before daylight, He went out and departed to a solitary place; and there He prayed. And Simon and those who were with Him searched for Him. When they found Him, they said to Him, "Everyone is looking for You." But He said to them, "Let us go into the next towns, that I may preach there also, because for this purpose I have come forth." And He was preaching in their synagogues throughout all Galilee, and casting out demons. Now a leper came to Him, imploring Him, kneeling down to Him and saying to Him, "If You are willing, You can make me clean." Then Jesus, moved with compassion, stretched out His hand and touched him, and said to him, "I am willing; be cleansed." As soon as He had spoken, immediately the leprosy left him, and he was cleansed.
>
> —MARK 1:30-42

When we look at the Bible, we see that both Jesus and God were willing to heal and deliver people, to teach and train people. The words "I will" are a powerful declaration. When we study the definition of the legal document called a will we see that it is the legal declaration of a person's wishes. When a will is written we know it is written precisely. It is legal and binding, and the executor has to execute the mandates of the will. It is similar to the word *will* in the Bible. When we look up the definition of the word *will* according to Webster's we discover that it can mean "a strong desire or determination." Our Father and Jesus, His Son, are determined to fulfill the commitment of the words they made in the Bible toward us and the words Jesus spoke while here as a man walking the earth.

Jesus encouraged them to follow Him and come to Him. He didn't say, "I may," or, "I might." He said, "I will."

> Then He said to them, "Follow Me, and I will make you fishers of men."
> —MATTHEW 4:19

> Come to Me, all you who labor and are heavy laden, and I will give you rest.
> —MATTHEW 11:28

Jesus kept His words about healing, confessing us before His Father and building His church.

> And Jesus said to him, "I will come and heal him."
> —MATTHEW 8:7

> Therefore whoever confesses Me before men, him I will also confess before My Father who is in heaven.
> —MATTHEW 10:32

> And I also say to you that you are Peter, and on
> this rock I will build My church, and the gates
> of Hades shall not prevail against it.
>
> —MATTHEW 16:18

Jesus empowered us by giving us the instructions for binding and loosing. The Father poured out His Spirit, the very Spirit that we are seeing manifest in the days of the kingdom, which are upon us.

> And I will give you the keys of the kingdom of
> heaven, and whatever you bind on earth will be
> bound in heaven, and whatever you loose on
> earth will be loosed in heaven.
>
> —MATTHEW 16:19

> And it shall come to pass in the last days, says
> God, That I will pour out of My Spirit on all
> flesh; Your sons and your daughters shall
> prophesy, Your young men shall see visions,
> Your old men shall dream dreams. And on my
> menservants and on my maidservants I will
> pour out My Spirit in those days; And they
> shall prophesy.
>
> —ACTS 2:17-18

Filler words in the Bible get little attention. However, words like *if, may, can, then, will,* and others have a mighty message to bring to us when read in the context of the entire passage.

Going back to the beginning of the Bible, we read that Adam was made out of the dust of the ground: "And the LORD God formed man of the dust of the ground, and breathed into his nostrils the breath of life, and man became a living being" (Gen. 2:7). If God created Adam out of the dust of the ground, then He can create anything with your words. Think of the magnitude here of what your God can do. He can take dust—dirt from the ground—create a human being, and breathe the breath of life into it. He can breathe the breath of life into your situation. All you have to do is speak to your situation. God is the ultimate Creator, and He has allowed us to establish and create things with our words. Out of nothing He formed Adam and this universe, and out of nothing He can form many things through your words. Empower yourself by being in the Word and learning what He established and how He gave you the same ability.

We too have the ability to create with our spoken words. In Romans it says that God called forth and created the earth from nothing: "('I have made you a father of many nations') in the presence of Him whom he believed—God, who gives life to the dead and calls those things which do not exist as though they did" (Rom. 4:17). God called nonexistent things into existence. As long as God has given us a word of knowledge and we know it is His will (which I discuss in more detail in another chapter), then we too can call nonexistent things into existence. Unlike God, we are not going to be able to create a person or car from the dust. However, we can call things that He has set aside for us in the spiritual realm into natural existence, such as a new home, job, promotion, etc.

In order to call those things forth we need to know from Scripture that we have the authority, and we have to know that if God spoke and created so can we. This kind of faith comes by building ourselves up in the Word of God and what the Bible says we can have. We need to see throughout the Bible where God created and things manifested with the out-spoken word. We must discover the authority that we have in and through Jesus. The Father spoke and created because He had authority. But in His Word it says that we have also been given authority.

> Then God said, "Let Us make man in Our image, according to Our likeness; let them have dominion over the fish of the sea, over the birds of the air, and over the cattle, over all the earth and over every creeping thing that creeps on the earth."
>
> —Genesis 1:26

> Behold, I give you the authority to trample on serpents and scorpions, and over all the power of the enemy, and nothing shall by any means hurt you.
>
> —Luke 10:19

God created Eve out of the bone of Adam: "And the LORD God caused a deep sleep to fall on Adam, and he slept; and He took one of his ribs, and closed up the flesh in its place. Then the rib which the Lord God had taken from man He made into a woman, and He brought her to the man" (Gen. 2:21-22). See how God created something into existence?

He formed all of the animals out of the dust of the ground: "Out of the ground the LORD God formed every beast of the field and every bird of the air, and brought them to Adam to see what he would call them. And whatever Adam called each living creature, that was its name" (Gen. 2:19). God created substance from nothing. He spoke into existence what had not existed previously.

We all have circumstances where something good needs to be called forth. Perhaps you have a rocky marriage or a wayward child. There are a multitude of good things we can declare into existence by speaking forth and proclaiming our prayers. Statements such as:

> *I command my marriage to be in strength and unity.*

> *I say my spouse and I will get along.*

> *I say my spouse and I will have Christ as the center of our marriage.*

> *I proclaim my child will come back to the Lord and walk with Him.*

> *I call forth conviction on my child and say the darkness will be exposed.*

Declaring isn't necessarily for a physical possession, though it can be. Declaring is praying something into existence that is God's desire but that you haven't seen manifested in the spiritual or natural realm. It could be for a loved one, as I gave examples above, or it could be for breaking free from depression, anger, or rejection, statements such as:

> *I command depression to leave my mind in Jesus' name.*

> *All heaviness, weight, and distraction in my soul be gone now in Jesus' name.*

> *I am not rejected by people because my acceptance comes from God.*

> *Anger can't live in me because the Bible says I have* shalom, *peace.*

Declaring these positive statements and declarations into existence over our lives can help renew our minds. As we speak these things in power, authority, and faith, the spirit realm must respond and listen to us. As we declare these things over our lives it also helps us to build faith so that we can renew our thought patterns. Speaking into existence those things that are not can affect your spiritual, natural, or emotional state. What do you need to start speaking out today?

If we can do the same things God can—and we can!—then we can call things forth into existence.

4
JESUS SPOKE, AND THINGS RESPONDED

THE FATHER DECLARED over Jesus, His Son, when Jesus was baptized. He made a public declaration and said, "This is My beloved Son" (Matt. 3:17). The Father also spoke things into existence in the very beginning in the Book of Genesis. The Father spoke to things and declared into the spiritual atmosphere. It is only natural that Jesus, one part of the Godhead, or Trinity, would also declare and speak to things.

Jesus came to Earth to give us authority. He desires His believers to be empowered, which is the reason why we receive the Holy Spirit. He also wants us to have victory, which is why He conquered the grave. Jesus came to Earth not only to give us our salvation, healing, and deliverance but to model how to live a life of strength, power, authority, and love.

Jesus spoke to things while on Earth. He instructed us to speak to our mountains. He spoke to blind eyes, storms, and fig trees. Jesus declared and decreed out what He wanted to manifest, and He saw the fruit of those spoken words. Through those words He released healing into a person's body, cast demons (spirit beings) out of bodies, and spoke to nature, and all of them responded.

Jesus spoke in faith! Jesus had faith! When we look at the life of Jesus we see He wasn't passive or lazy. Complacency has struck the body of Christ and paralyzed them. Due to passivity and lack of motivation, ambition, or real desire to make a change, the body of Christ hasn't been empowered to truly pray! Christians don't want to rise up and pray as they should and take authority over situations. Many times this is the case simply because they don't feel like it or haven't been taught how. However, when we look at Jesus, those hindrances never struck Him. He kept moving forward despite opposition, which is the definition of perseverance. He knew time was short, that the kingdom was at hand, and that He had to be about His Father's business. We could all learn a lesson from Jesus about the way He pursued people, showed love to people, and was about kingdom building. If you want to be like Jesus study how He acted and who He was in the gospels. See for yourself that the power you hold and the ministry you engage in can be similar to that of Jesus Christ.

When Jesus was being tempted in the desert He showed the power of speaking the written word out of our mouth: "But He answered and said, 'It is written, "Man shall not live by bread alone, but by every word that proceeds from the mouth of God"'" (Matt. 4:4). Jesus fought with the Word, with the out-spoken Word. In Matthew 4:1-11 each time the devil tempted Jesus He struck back with the Word. He spoke to things.

> Then Jesus was led up by the Spirit into the wilderness to be tempted by the devil. And when He had fasted forty days and forty

nights, afterward He was hungry. Now when the tempter came to Him, he said, "If You are the Son of God, command that these stones become bread." But He answered and said, "It is written, 'Man shall not live by bread alone, but by every word that proceeds from the mouth of God.'" Then the devil took Him up into the holy city, set Him on the pinnacle of the temple, and said to Him, "If You are the Son of God, throw Yourself down. For it is written: 'He shall give his angels charge over you,' and, 'In their hands they shall bear you up, Lest you dash your foot against a stone.'" Jesus said to him, "It is written again, 'You shall not tempt the LORD your God.'" Again, the devil took Him up on an exceedingly high mountain and showed Him all the kingdoms of the world and their glory. And he said to Him, "All these things I will give You if You will fall down and worship me." Then Jesus said to him, "Away with you, Satan! For it is written, 'You shall worship the LORD your God, and Him only you shall serve.'" Then the devil left Him, and behold, angels came and ministered to Him.

—MATTHEW 4:1-11

One of the interesting things I find about this passage is the fact that the devil instructed Jesus to command when he said, "Command that these stones become bread" (v. 3). Did the devil himself know the power of commanding? I believe he did. The devil could hear how Jesus ministered and spoke to things while He was here on the earth. When casting out demons, even the demons asked Him not to command them where to go: "And they begged Him that He would not command them to go out into the abyss" (Luke 8:31). I believe they knew the power of His words and commands.

Jesus knew the power of speaking out. That is why He used His words and the Word of God to combat the tactics of the enemy. We too need to use our words. We use them in everything else. We like to talk about our situations all the time; instead of talking about them, we need to talk to them.

We read in the Gospels that Jesus declared and decreed to things. Just look at all of the red-letter words that are in the Bible, which are actual words that Jesus spoke. These were declarations, simple statements where He was giving orders and instructions, such as:

- "Go!" (Matt. 8:32).

- "Great is your faith! Let it be [done] to you" (Matt. 15:28).

- "Get behind Me, Satan!" (Matt. 16:23).

- "Be quiet, and come out of him!" (Mark 1:25).

- "Come out of the man, unclean spirit" (Mark 5:8).

- "You are loosed from your infirmity" (Luke 13:12).

- "Loose him, and let him go" (John 11:44).

Look at the results of these simple statements He made and the commands He gave. A woman was healed of an affliction she had put up with for years. A man, who had been in a cave tormented by a demon for a very long time, making him violent and crazy, sat peacefully in his right mind. People were healed, delivered, and set free! Hallelujah! Praise You, Jesus!

When we know the love of God and it permeates our heart, we will know that it is His desire for us to speak to things. We will know the heart of the Father.

> Jesus said to him, "You shall love the LORD your God with all your heart, with all your soul, and with all your mind."
>
> —MATTHEW 22:37

Because Jesus knew the Father's heart He also knew the power of the Scriptures and the power of God.

> Jesus answered and said to them, "You are mistaken, not knowing the Scriptures nor the power of God."
>
> —MATTHEW 22:29

He spoke because He knew the power it contained.

Jesus reached out with compassion, love, faith, and authority, releasing His healing power into people. With the paralytic man, He not only healed him, but He forgave his sins. He spoke to him, and the paralytic got up and walked out of that place.

> "But that you may know that the Son of Man has power on earth to forgive sins"—then He said to the paralytic, "Arise, take up your bed, and go to your house."
>
> —MATTHEW 9:6

He spoke into the spiritual atmosphere, the spirit realm responded, and the paralytic man's condition left him.

With the little girl He spoke a simple statement of faith, "Arise," and she was made well.

> But He put them all outside, took her by the hand and called, saying, "Little girl, arise."
>
> —Luke 8:54

He did not pray in the following manner: "Oh, heavenly Father, please heal her. This is Your daughter, and I know You love her." He didn't go on and on, begging, pleading, and petitioning. He went to her house in faith, knowing that the Father would accomplish His perfect will, which is to heal. He spoke a simple statement of faith, and she arose and lived!

In the case of the woman with the blood issue Jesus again spoke into the atmosphere, and her condition left her: "But Jesus turned around, and when He saw her He said, 'Be of good cheer, daughter; your faith has made you well.' And the woman was made well from that hour" (Matt. 9:22). The spiritual realm responded immediately. She was made well from that hour, as He felt the healing virtue leave Him. All of this occurred from simply speaking into the atmosphere, speaking to body parts and conditions, and telling them to line up with the Word of God.

It is God's desire to heal you. Jesus came to purchase your healing. Instead of talking about your condition, why not try decreeing and declaring to your condition? Tell your body parts to line up with the Word of God. Speak to your bone marrow, and tell it to function properly. Command your blood to be purified. Call forth T-cells to eat up and destroy that cancer attacking your body. Tell the serotonin levels in your head to be normal, and command those headaches to go in Jesus' name. Stop praying about your medical condition and start speaking to it.

Jesus commanded paralyzed people to get up and take up their mat, withered arms and hands to be normal, leprosy to be healed, and blind eyes to open. If He can command them and have them come into alignment with the Word of God and be perfected again, and if He can call forth creative miracles to heal and restore, so can we. We can do it; the problem is that we don't do it. Activate your faith, and expect the unexpected. Expect the possible to happen, because with Jesus all things are possible. Take action, stand in faith, and believe to receive the complete manifestation of your healing through the out-spoken Word of God and the words of your faith decreed into your body.

Declare healing Scriptures over the conditions and parts of your body that need to be healed. If there is an eye challenge you are facing, then rely on these Scriptures:

The eyes of those who see will not be dim.
—ISAIAH 32:3

But blessed are your eyes for they see, and your ears for they hear.
—MATTHEW 13:16

By His stripes, I am healed!
—ISAIAH 53:5, AUTHOR'S PARAPHRASE

Claim out these scriptural declarations. You could say:

My eyes will not be dim.

I shall have perfect, 20/20 vision.

Eyes, come into alignment with the Word, which says you see. Now, see clearly, without being inhibited!

My eyes are working in the perfection that my Father made them in.

Cornea, optical nerve, retinas, work properly, in Jesus' name.

Jesus commanded things to leave, took authority over them, and then gave them a command.

> When Jesus saw that the people came running together, He rebuked the unclean spirit, saying to it: "Deaf and dumb spirit, I command you, come out of him and enter him no more!"
>
> —MARK 9:25

He commanded the spirit to come out and then gave it an order or directive to enter him no more. Jesus didn't pray for the spirit to come out. He didn't have people engage in hours of repetitive prayers of renouncement, like a lot of inner healing and deliverance models call for. He simply took authority over this demon and cast it out. If we would declare and take authority, many more people could be delivered. Many Christians have been taught the wrong deliverance model and have not followed the example Jesus Christ set for us. Yes, it is important to forgive, but it is not biblical to sit for six to eight hours in a ministry chair ritually and legalistically renouncing and repenting! Show me where that is in the Bible. Jesus took authority! He rebuked the demon and cast it out, and the person was delivered. Yes, we need to give teaching and instruction to the person. Teaching and inner healing are vital parts of deliverance ministry, but casting the demons out and getting right down to business, as Jesus did, is more effective and the biblical model that we should be following. He declared, and it left.

I believe that since even our deliverance ministers haven't been taught the power of declaring they spend too much time caught up in a man-made plan rather than relying on the instruction of the Holy Spirit and listening to what He tells them to do in a session. If you doubt what I am saying here, please search the Scriptures and test the spirits. Search out how Jesus engaged in deliverance. I have been a deliverance minister for years, and we simply do not have time to spend hours upon hours in repentant renunciation prayers that become legalistic and ritualistic. I have found that such prayers have little meaning because people are just repeating prayers to get the job done instead of really meaning them. After they spend hours doing this it becomes redundant, and they start feeling numb and bored and just want to get on with it. How do I know? Those people eventually come to me after their sessions with others because they did not gain freedom. They truly believe in demons and are just seeking someone who will cast them out. Do what Jesus did. Cast them out!

Don't fall short in what you want to command and accomplish. People think you can simply rebuke the devil and repeatedly say, "I rebuke you, devil. I rebuke you, devil." *To rebuke* simply means "to take authority over." When Jesus rebuked the devil He gave him an instruction:

> But He turned and rebuked them, and said, "You
> do not know what manner of spirit you are of."
> —LUKE 9:55

But Jesus rebuked him, saying, "Be quiet, and come out of him!" And when the demon had thrown him in their midst, it came out of him and did not hurt him.

—Luke 4:35

But when He had turned around and looked at His disciples, He rebuked Peter, saying, "Get behind Me, Satan! For you are not mindful of the things of God, but the things of men."

—Mark 8:33

When Jesus saw that the people came running together, He rebuked the unclean spirit, saying to it, "Deaf and dumb spirit, I command you, come out of him and enter him no more!"

—Mark 9:25

He spoke to that demon sternly and authoritatively: "For He said to him, 'Come out of the man, unclean spirit!'" (Mark 5:8). If someone talked to you sternly and with authority, most likely you would be scared, have a little fear rise up, and respond. If that person were in a position of authority, such as a military or police officer, and they gave you an authoritative instruction, you would snap up, listen, and obey. You would respond, believing that they mean business. Yes, that is the kind of reaction your words should get!

When Jesus called Lazarus out of the grave, he lived!

And he who had died came out bound hand and foot with graveclothes, and his face was wrapped with a cloth. Jesus said to them, "Loose him, and let him go."

—John 11:44

What is dead in your life that you need to call forth? In Ezekiel we are instructed to prophesy and speak to those dry bones (Ezek. 37:4). Is your marriage dead, your child wayward, or your business in distress? Call those things that are not as though they are (Rom. 4:17). Speak to the marriage and tell it to come into unity and be restored in Jesus' name. Proclaim that your spouse and marriage will not be a dead carcass for the enemy to feed on, but it has the life and love of Jesus flowing through it! Quote out scriptures about the prodigal son who came home, and claim that for your children. Proclaim that your house will serve the Lord and that your children will not depart from the way you have trained them.

Speak! Declare it into the spiritual atmosphere! Do not remain silent! Get violent, and activate your faith. Put forth the sword of the Spirit, the Word of God, which is sharper than a two-edged sword. That two-edged sword is contingent on you. On one side is the Word of God that we put into ourselves, and on the other side is that very same Word of God that we put out to others. We need both parts. Remember that you can only put out what you put in. Therefore, be in the Word of God, and put the Scriptures into your soul and spirit. But also, speak out the Scriptures. Memorize them so that you can combat the devil with them and declare and decree over your children, finances, health, ministry, and for every good and prosperous thing that God has for you.

The enemy will try to come and rob and destroy everything that God has set aside for you. The devil knows your prophecies, and when he knows them he is going to try and destroy them. He wants to demolish every good and perfect gift. He wants to destroy everything that God has set to establish. That is why you have to be vigilant in speaking the Word and watching for any distractions in your normal, everyday life. He will try to disrupt and disturb everything that God has planned. The time is now to rise up and speak to each and every situation, as you see here. It does not have to be in fifteen-minute or thirty-minute increments. Jesus simply let out six words, which were powerful words: "Loose him, and let him go" (John 11:44). When is the last time you said that about your spouse or children?

PROPHETIC PRAYER DECLARATION

Devil, loose them and let them go! I bind and restrict you from attacking my family, and I cover them with the blood of Christ. No weapon formed against them will prosper. No sickness and plague will come near their dwelling. They live in the shelter of the Most High. You can't have them, devil, so get off. Get away. I bind and restrict you and tell you to abort your assignment against my family, because they have been sealed into the sonship of Jesus Christ. They have a kingdom inheritance, and all things evil are under their feet. They are seated and positioned in heavenly places, have an army of angels at their disposal, and you, devil, are a defeated foe. You lose. You've lost, and you are going to burn for eternity.

Get away from my family. I'm taking authority over them. I'm claiming them for the kingdom; for them to walk in their rightful positions; for them to rise up and take authority, spiritual leadership, and to seek and pursue God. I say and decree that they will serve God all the days of their lives. They will prosper in everything they set their hands to. God has given them divine favor. They have an overflowing cup and a portion of their inheritance, and you, devil, will not steal, kill, or destroy what God has intended for them.

Devil, I call off your plans to abort and abolish the plans of God in my family's life, and I burn your plans up with the fire of God. I release the love and power of God into their situation to conquer any obstacles. There will be no hindrances in my family's path, but God will go before us. We will not look to the left or right, but straight ahead and keep looking forward with eager expectation for the plans and purposes of God to manifest in our lives. I seal them into the kingdom of God so that no weapon formed against them will prosper.

I say God's Word will go forth in their lives and will accomplish what He pleases it to accomplish. My family will be an instrument of Your peace, to accomplish Your will and the great and mighty plans that you have for them. I call forth my family members to receive the conviction and instruction of the Holy Spirit and to walk in and activate that plan with no delays in their assignment.

> *I call this prophetic declaration forth and seal*
> *it in with the blood of Christ. I call forth angels*
> *to dispatch and activate on this declaration*
> *released by the Holy Spirit through the spirit of*
> *revelation, in Jesus' name. Amen.*

Now when is the last time you prayed like that? That is the way we should be binding and restricting the devil. We should be reading this and declaring it out. The Holy Spirit downloaded that prophetic declaration as I was writing this chapter, and since He is no respecter of persons He can do for you what He can do for me. But you have to make yourself available. Are you available? Are you obedient to Him? Do you sit and listen? Do you take the time to receive the downloads and instructions and revelation that He longs to give you? You do not receive revelation sometimes because you won't quiet yourself and get in His presence, slow down from the busyness, stop doing things, and make yourself available. Be available, and He will show up and give you a prophetic declaration that specifically applies to your situation.

Jesus said when healing the blind man, "What do you want Me to do for you?" (Mark 10:36). I believe Jesus was modeling the power of our words. All through the Bible we read about the out-spoken word. We are told to speak to our mountains, that death and life are in the power of the tongue, and to call things that are not as though they are. (See Matthew 17:20; Proverbs 18:21; Romans 4:17.) We need to align our words and actions up with our faith.

Do we have a part to play in our healing? When Jesus went to heal a man, He said, "Stretch out your hand" (Mark 3:5). The man took a prophetic action and lined up his faith in the natural by stretching out his hand. Do your words line up? Think about the amount of words we speak and actions we take in a day. Are they lining up with the spiritual, prophetic action that Jesus wants us to take?

Jesus was putting this man's faith to action, a prophetic action. He was making the man speak what He wanted. There is power in our words. The blind man said, "That I may receive my sight" (Mark 10:51). The statement, "That I may receive my sight," was a declaration. He was declaring and speaking into the spiritual atmosphere what he wanted to manifest in the natural realm. Declaring is powerful! The Word says, "Declare a thing, and it shall come to pass" (Job 22:28, author's paraphrase). Of course, we know that it comes to pass when it is the Father's will. The blind man didn't say, "Please pray for my eyes. I want to see." He declared out what he wanted!

I learned an important lesson from the prophet I mentioned in a previous chapter. For months I kept telling everyone I knew that he would be my spiritual father. I kept saying, "I will have him as my spiritual father. God, I want that man as my spiritual father." I didn't pray with eloquent words. I simply stated what I wanted and believed. I claimed it. I commanded it. I decreed it! When I finally sat down at the table with him I didn't even have to bring it up. He asked me, "What do you want? What have you been asking of God?" He knew the answer. The heavenly Father had prepared his heart. This man was in communication with the Father, and he told me, "God knows what you want"—and so did he!—"but you have to ask for it." The Father wants you to ask for things of Him. Take prophetic action and speak your desires out, like Jesus made the blind man do.

Remember, God loves to give spiritual gifts. Speak out! What do you want Jesus to do for you? Put your natural circumstance into a prophetic proclamation and believe for your situation to change.

Jesus modeled for us how He commanded nature, and nature obeyed Him.

> And seeing a fig tree by the road, He came to it and found nothing on it but leaves, and said to it, "Let no fruit grow on you ever again." Immediately the fig tree withered away.
> —MATTHEW 21:19

> Then He arose and rebuked the wind, and said to the sea, "Peace, be still!" And the wind ceased, and there was a great calm.
> —MARK 4:39

Jesus spoke to a fig tree, and nature responded to what He said. Can you even imagine that? Nature responded to Jesus, and nature can respond to you! When He spoke to the sea and rebuked the wind, again, He modeled what we can be doing. When storms come to our area the first thing my husband and I do is speak to the wind, storms, trees, our property, and possessions. We command the storm to cease around our home and trees not to blow down or limbs to break off. We command our pool to be undamaged and no roof damage to occur in Jesus' name. After the storms have left there have been times when our neighbors had branches down or home damage, and our house has always been left untouched.

Did you ever stop to consider that Jesus' last words were a declaration: "So when Jesus had received the sour wine, He said, "It is finished!" And bowing His head, He gave up His spirit" (John 19:30)? It is finished! He declared those powerful words out of His mouth. Again, He didn't pray, "Oh, Father, take up my Spirit," or anything like that. He considered the work of the cross and the work He did complete. He gave up His Spirit in faith and declared, "It is finished."

There is another piece of Scripture that I don't think we are fully aware is a declaration; it is the Lord's Prayer (Matt. 6:9-13). The Lord's Prayer consists of simple statements spoken in faith. When we look at the Book of Luke, the disciples were asking Jesus to teach them how to pray. When Jesus responded, He said, "When you pray, say..." Notice the word *say*. Jesus instructed them to say; He did not tell them to think or pray in their mind but said, "When you pray, say..."

> Now it came to pass, as He was praying in a certain place, when He ceased, that one of His disciples said to Him, "Lord, teach us to pray, as John also taught his disciples." So He said to them, "When you pray, say: Our Father in heaven, Hallowed be Your name. Your kingdom come. Your will be done On earth as it is in heaven. Give us day by day our daily bread. And forgive us our sins, For we also forgive everyone who is indebted to us. And do not lead us into temptation, But deliver us from the evil one."
> —LUKE 11:1-4

As I was studying this I was reading different versions of the Bible. *The Message* version, with its simple sentence structure, shows how this can be understood as a declaration.

> This is your Father you are dealing with, and he knows better than you what you need. With a God like this loving you, you can pray very

simply. Like this: Our Father in heaven, Reveal who you are. Set the world right; Do what's best—as above, so below. Keep us alive with three square meals. Keep us forgiven with you and forgiving others. Keep us safe from ourselves and the Devil. You're in charge! You can do anything you want! You're ablaze in beauty! Yes. Yes. Yes.

—MATTHEW 6:8-13, THE MESSAGE

Would you pray this in your mind? No! This is powerful! It needs to be spoken out! The Bible was intended to be read aloud to others, to be read and spoken. In Old Testament times they didn't have a Bible in print to read. However, when I read this, it ignites me. The out-spoken Word of God ignites you because faith comes by hearing. When you hear what you say, your faith is ignited!

The original text of the Complete Jewish Bible translates the Lord's Prayer like this:

You, therefore, pray like this: "Our Father in heaven! May your Name be kept holy. May your Kingdom come, your will be done on earth as in heaven. Give us the food we need today. Forgive us what we have done wrong, as we too have forgiven those who have wronged us. And do not lead us into hard testing, but keep us safe from the Evil One. For kingship, power and glory are yours forever. Amen."

—MATTHEW 6:9-13, CJB

"May your Name be kept holy"—that is declaring! It is calling forth the kingdom and His will. We should all be praying out loud like that. Think of what could manifest on Earth if we took our passion and love for the Lord and declared out His prayer with enthusiasm and expectation!

When Jesus prayed, do you think He prayed out loud or silently in His mind? Jesus had a deep relationship with His Father. If you have a deep relationship with someone, you talk to them. You don't try to read each other's minds or communicate telepathically, which as Christians we definitely should not be doing since that is a form of witchcraft. My point is that you talk to the person. You don't attempt to have a conversation connected in the soul or spirit. You verbally communicate.

Jesus knew the importance of communicating. He was in one of His deepest moments of despair, and He went to pray and talk to His Father. He desired communication and relationship to the Father, so He knelt down and spoke with Him. He shared His concerns, grief, and anguish with Him.

> And He was withdrawn from them about a stone's throw, and He knelt down and prayed, saying, "Father, if it is Your will, take this cup away from Me; nevertheless not My will, but Yours, be done." Then an angel appeared to Him from heaven, strengthening Him. And being in agony, He prayed more earnestly. Then His sweat became like great drops of blood falling down to the ground.
>
> —LUKE 22:41-44

Jesus was in such agony that He sweat blood. Imagine that—praying so hard, being so crushed in the spirit and the soul, that He sweat blood. Most of us don't even pray so hard that we sweat through our clothes, yet He sweat blood. Do you think if He was in that kind of agony and

101

distress that He could effectively pray in His mind to the Father? Of course not! A conversation like that had to have taken place verbally.

You may be thinking that your situation is different and that you're not in agony, as Jesus was. No, you may not be in agony. But aren't we supposed to be like Jesus? He came to Earth to model how to live a life that is honoring and pleasing to the Father and so that He could know everything we experience. Jesus gave the disciples the Lord's Prayer when they asked Him how to pray. Don't you think Jesus praying in the garden could have been another model and chance for them to learn how to pray? After all, Jesus took them to the garden with Him. He said, "Could you not watch with Me one hour?" (Matt. 26:40). He came and found them sleeping. Jesus was on a prayer watch. He took His disciples with Him. Instead of praying with Him, watching, staying awake, or whatever He wanted them to do, He discovered them sleeping! This is the way we also find people today, bored and tired with their prayer life and not praying. They instead leave it up to everyone else to pray for them. The disciples could have learned from the greatest Intercessor, yet they chose to comfort their flesh instead of growing their spiritual life and learning from Jesus Himself.

What we learn about Jesus praying in the garden is that He had to have His mind, soul, emotions, spirit, and flesh connected. He was connected to the Father Spirit to Spirit, but the rest of Him was also in the game, so to speak. He cried out, "If it is Your will, take this cup away from Me; nevertheless not My will, but Yours, be done" (Luke 22:42). Even though His flesh was uncomfortable, He still submitted His will to God's will and kept the focus on the end prize for all people.

We learn a lesson from Jesus here that it is not about us. It is about others. He kept the focus on His Father's will and the redemption of all mankind. We as people cannot always remove our selfishness and desire for comfort for the benefit of others. This affects our prayer life too. When we don't know how to pray we sometimes give up instead of pressing in for those who need our prayer. We are uncomfortable, but we need to submit our flesh and come into alignment with God's will. This can be done by speaking prayers out loud through declaring. Most of us have grown up without being taught to speak out our prayers, but we need to step out of our comfort zone and prepare our heart and mind that our prayers do get answered by praying differently than we have before.

Trying something new tends to be scary and unfamiliar to people. To you it may sound weird to start praying out loud and declaring. However, if Jesus communicated with the Father that way and spoke to things, so should we. What do you have to lose by trying it? Your reputation, if someone hears you? They may just join you! When we are really sold out for Christ we lose our reputation a thousand times over anyway. Try speaking to things. You may just find yourself ignited by a new way to pray, and you may discover that you just can't stop praying.

5
DOES YOUR
FAITH LINE UP?

THERE IS PROMISE and power in God's Word. We have to put our faith with it to ignite it. Do you have faith, or are you in faith? Having faith isn't enough. A lot of people have faith. What is needed is to be manifesting that faith. Being in faith is believing that you can receive and believing what the Word of God says is for you and not just everyone else.

It is easier to believe for someone else's miracle or blessing than your own. When you pray for healing for a person you believe that person is going to be healed. When someone prays healing for you or you pray healing for yourself you don't always have that same faith. It is the same with finances, a miracle, desiring a child, or expecting a promotion; most people can believe it will happen for another person but doubt it will happen for them. The reality of what has happened in your life in the past may have been unfruitful. Therefore, since you didn't receive in the past you doubt that you can receive in the future.

To declare, you need to establish your faith to line up with the will and Word of God. Believe that the same God who desired to bless people in the Bible desires to bless you! The Scripture shows us that He is a God who desires to give good gifts to His children (Matt. 7:11). He desires to give good gifts to all of His children; that includes you! Believe you can receive.

In order to increase your faith you need to build your faith by reading and studying the Scriptures and what they say about faith. It is not enough to read the Bible; you need to study it, dissect it, and digest it. You need to know what the Bible says about faith and how to apply it to your life. After all, the Bible is the greatest book of faith!

You start building your faith by removing the old teachings you received that did not line up with the Word of God. These are teachings you received that were legalistic and didn't preach the complete victory that the Bible says we can have. There are teachings we have all received that conveyed to us that, as Christians, we aren't supposed to live in prosperity. Pastors and church leaders have taught us we need to live in poverty and deprivation. We have been instructed to live without instead of with, and we have even been looked down upon if we had much. This is stinking thinking! Our God doesn't want us living in lack but abundance. His Word even states that He came to give us life in abundance (John 10:10). Let's start abundant and fruitful living!

Search out the Scriptures on prosperity and abundance. Read about the blessings He desires to bestow upon us. Don't allow legalistic teaching from your past to prevent your present or future blessing.

Root out and destroy any thoughts that you are not worthy of such a blessing. Unworthiness will destroy the manifestation of your blessing because you won't have the mentality that you deserve it. When you remain in a victim mentality you don't know how to be a victor. It is imperative to change your perceptions and what you believed in the past, to replace your old thoughts with new revelation.

To receive the blessing on the other side of the declaration you need to remove any inability to receive. Christians have a receiving problem. It is rooted in unworthiness. When you don't feel worthy you don't know how to receive. You are worthy because Jesus is worthy, and He lives in you. That is the plain simplicity of the gospel, and until you come to that realization there will be stumbling blocks and obstacles. Clear your pathway and remove everything that hinders you from receiving the blessings of God.

Align your words and your actions with your faith. Jesus caused a man to manifest his faith to be healed when Jesus said, "Stretch out your hand" (Mark 3:5). The man performed a prophetic action to line up his faith in the natural by stretching out his hand. Do your words line up? Do your actions line up? Think about the amount of words spoken and actions taken in a day. Are they lining up with the spiritual, prophetic action that Jesus wants us to take?

There is power in our words. When asked what he wanted Christ to do for him, the blind man said, "That I may receive my sight" (Luke 18:41). The words *that I may receive sight* were a declaration. He was declaring and speaking into the spiritual atmosphere what he wanted to manifest in the natural realm. Declaring is powerful! The Word says, "Declare a thing, and it shall come to pass" (Job 22:28, author's paraphrase). Of course, we know that occurs when it is the Father's will. The blind man didn't say, "Please pray for my eyes. I want to see." He declared out what he wanted!

This reminds me of a time when I was diagnosed with needing a root canal and a crown. I thought, "Really, God, I know of a better way to spend two thousand dollars of your money." I stood in faith for months to receive my healing. I stated to the dentist right at the time of diagnosis that my God was going to heal me. He laughed and said, "Those things don't go away by themselves, you know." I stood in faith! I went to the altar one day, and I stated what I wanted. I said, "I want God to heal my tooth so that no root canal is needed." I didn't ask for prayer. I claimed what I wanted the result to be. You know what I received? A doctor's report verified by three tests and one X-ray that showed I didn't need any root canal! Glory to God! Everywhere I went and every time I saw someone I declared to them that I would be healed! I also spoke to the tooth to be healed!

James says, "But let him ask in faith, with no doubting, for he who doubts is like a wave of the sea driven and tossed by the wind" (James 1:6). I believed, had faith, and declared and received my blessing. However, even more than personally receiving my healing, I received a testimony through which Jesus' name could be glorified, and I could encourage others through the power of declaring.

I had to stand on my faith, and that is what you need to do when God is calling you to do so. We know it is His will to heal, and that could be one of the places where you need to build your faith. Therefore, speak to your condition, tell it to come into alignment with the Word of God, and have the faith that it will.

The Bible tells us that we will have what we seek if we can believe we will receive.

And whatever things you ask in prayer, believing, you will receive.

—MATTHEW 21:22

Therefore I say to you, whatever things you ask when you pray, believe that you receive them, and you will have them.

—MARK 11:24

It is not enough to ask or declare. You need to believe by faith and trust in Yeshua Messiah that you will receive. He loves to hear His children talk to Him and ask Him by faith. Ask. Don't be like a wave of the sea (James 1:6). Be still and be sure of what you are asking. Confirm it in prayer. Have the Spirit of the Lord verify that what you are asking is in accordance with His will. Once you have confirmation, then ask without doubting in your heart. If you know it is His will it will manifest. You just don't know the timing.

Faith takes perseverance. Perseverance is continuing forward despite opposition. The opposition could be our own doubt and unbelief. Root out doubt and unbelief at its very core. Make doubt and unbelief wash out into the sea instead of your faith being washed out into the sea.

God "is a rewarder of those who diligently seek Him" (Heb. 11:6). If you are going to seek Him for something that is going to edify His kingdom, why wouldn't He want to bless you with it?

But without faith, it is impossible to please Him, for he who comes to God must believe that He is, and that He is a rewarder of those who diligently seek Him.

—HEBREWS 11:6

You have a choice to make. You can be without faith or with faith. The Complete Jewish Bible uses the word *trust* in this verse instead of the word *faith*. You could say: You can be with trust that God will accomplish it, or you can be without trust. Do you want to be in a place of trust or distrust? Of course, you desire to trust. You just don't always know how to get to that place of trust, and, coincidentally, that is what this chapter is about.

The centurion who encountered Jesus had trust and knew the power of declaring what he wanted to happen. He "answered and said, 'Lord, I am not worthy that You should come under my roof. But only speak a word, and my servant will be healed'" (Matt. 8:8). The centurion activated his faith and trust by physically going to find Jesus. This was a prophetic action of faith. He knew there was healing to take place. He knew Jesus had the power and authority to do it. Now he had to go and declare to the One who could make it happen. In this passage we see that the centurion knew and had faith. You have to know and have faith. He also spoke out in a declaration what would happen, and it did! His servant was healed!

The woman with the blood issue also made a declaration of faith and took a prophetic action: "For she said, 'If only I may touch His clothes, I shall be made well'" (Mark 5:28). Her first action of faith, which I call a prophetic action, is that she pursued Jesus. She pushed through the crowd. She could have aimed to hug Him, to embrace Him, but her expectations were full of faith when she said, "If only I may touch His clothes." She had the faith of a giant. Her faith was giant because she wasn't expecting a great encounter with Him but only to touch His clothes. Her giant faith expected complete healing. She aligned her faith with her prophetic action to push through the crowds and believe that when she took the prophetic action to touch His clothes she would be healed. She made a declaration of her faith. She had faith to know that she would be healed if only she would touch His clothes.

She interrupted someone else's miracle to do it. Jesus was on His way to perform another miracle, not hers, but she had faith to reach in and grab what was hers. I also had a time like that. When I was seeking the healing of my tooth I actually had two teeth that were flaring up. I was having the kind of reaction you get to root pain, heat sensitivity that sends you shooting out of your chair. I was at my friend's conference, and he was calling for us to pray for other people. A group of us began to pray over a person for a tooth condition, and the person wasn't receiving. We were standing there, and I thought, "I will take this healing for myself." I put my hand on my mouth and started declaring over my mouth. At the very end of the night my friend again called out healings and just threw them up in the air like fireworks. One of them he called forth was dental miracles. I physically reached my arm up into the atmosphere and said, "I'll take that miracle." I took my hand and slapped that miracle on my mouth.

Afterward my husband and I went out to eat, and I could feel the power of God upon me. In the following days all of the pain and sensitivity I had in that tooth disappeared. I even had my dentist take an X-ray of it a couple of weeks later when I was in for a standard checkup, and there was no sign of anything being wrong. I believed. I took a prophetic action by taking that miracle and saw the manifestation. As I stated earlier, an X-ray of another tooth showed an abscess. That was also healed with a verified doctor's report. I stood in faith for the healing of two teeth and received what I declared out.

Each time I felt pain manifest in my body I declared out by faith, "By His stripes I am healed" (1 Pet. 2:24, author's paraphrase). I would speak to my pain and tell it to go in Jesus' name. I would command inflammation to leave in the name of Jesus. There is power in the name of Jesus! You too can command in faith for your body to align with the Word of God.

As the woman who touched Jesus' garment received her healing, Jesus reiterated to her that her activated faith had made her well: "He said to her, 'Daughter, your faith has made you well. Go in peace, and be healed of your affliction'" (Mark 5:34). She didn't just have faith; she was in faith! Think about faith this way. *Having* faith is like the frame of a door, but being *in* faith is walking through the door and closing the door behind you, enclosing yourself in faith.

Jesus encouraged belief as the ruler of the synagogue was coming to have his child raised from the dead: "As soon as Jesus heard the word that was spoken, He said to the ruler of the synagogue, 'Do not be afraid; only believe'" (Mark 5:36). Jesus even went a step further and only allowed His closest three disciples—James, Peter, and John—to follow Him into the room. Jesus wanted anyone with doubt and unbelief out of the room when He said, "Little girl, I say to you, arise" (v. 41).

When you believe in faith for something and you are making a declaration you want to be surrounded by those who have the same or greater faith than you do. You want to be surrounded by crazy-faith friends who will stand and believe with you. Do you have giant-faith friends who will lower your mat through the roof?

"Now some men brought in a bed a man who was paralyzed. They searched for ways to bring him in and lay him before Him. When they could not find a way to bring him in, because of the crowd, they went up on the roof and let him down through the tiles with his bed into their midst before Jesus. When He saw their faith, He said to him, "Man, your sins are forgiven you."
—LUKE 5:18-20, MEV

I love this story. The room, the house was full. This man's buddies were not going to let their friend *not* be healed. Not only did he receive his healing, but he received his deliverance. They had giant faith, crazy faith. They peeled apart the roof and lowered their buddy down. They were not going to take no for an answer.

We need to surround ourselves with the same kind of crazy-faith friends, friends who will stand by us when we believe for the impossible, because God's Word says, "If you can believe, all things are possible to him who believes" (Mark 9:23, MEV). When disease plagues us, divorce papers are served, and employment challenges arise we need friends who will stand in crazy faith with us and believe for what the world would consider impossible. We need friends who will stand strong for us and with us when times get tough, job losses happen, or a child reveals an unplanned pregnancy or addiction. We need crazy-faith friends who will encourage us and pray with us for hours on end to make the impossible possible. We need friends who will declare in faith with us and will stand in faith on what the Word of God says, that it is His desire to restore marriages, heal our bodies, and provide financial provision through employment. We need people who will stand with us to know our God will say yes when the world says no.

Jesus had such friends. He had a close disciple who was leaning on Him: "Now there was leaning on Jesus' bosom one of His disciples, whom Jesus loved" (John 13:23). The disciple leaning on Jesus, scholars believe, was probably John. Jesus had that one close friend like we have our best friends, mentors, or accountability partners. Jesus, then, had three that He allowed in His inner circle. The three were James, Peter, and John, as we see in Mark 5. He put all of the other people out of the room except the mother and father and His closest circle when He raised the little girl from the dead. (See Mark 5:35-43.)

Who do you want to stand beside you in a time of need? Who do you want to walk alongside you on a journey that you don't even want to take? What about when those divorce papers get served, the cancer diagnosis manifests, or the death of a loved one unexpectedly happens? Who do you want alongside you believing for the miraculous things the Bible tells us we can have? Who do you want standing in faith with you for the dead to be raised, healing to manifest, and that marriage to be restored? As the paralyzed man had crazy-faith friends to pull the roof off of a packed-out house and get him to Jesus for healing, who are going to be the crazy-faith friends who do some things that may cost them their reputation, inspiring them to do the impossible and encourage you along your way to victory? Hanging out with some crazy-faith friends will assist you in increasing your faith.

Jesus confirmed that the centurion only had to believe: "Jesus said to him, 'If you can believe, all things are possible to him who believes'" (Mark 9:23). That is why lining your faith up with your declaration and internal belief system is crucial. "If you can [only] believe…" Obviously you have some belief, which is why you are reading this book.

We need to grow deeply in our faith, renewing our mind daily. We need to speak to ourselves and our situation and state that we have been delivered from the kingdom of darkness into the kingdom of light. Now, we walk by faith and live in faith. We need to be constantly renewing our mind because the devil attempts to distract us several times a day to get us to move out of faith and into doubt and unbelief.

The Word tells us that "out of the abundance of the heart his mouth speaks" (Luke 6:45). When you decree, the knowledge you've stored inside becomes effective through your words. It is dependent upon the amount of Scripture you've stored up. You can only speak out what you have taken in and what is in your heart. If you don't believe what you read, then the knowledge may be in your mind, but it is not in your heart. Things are transferred to your heart when you speak them out. Truly, what is inside of us is what we will speak out; therefore, we are sometimes better off keeping our mouth shut.

When we read the Bible we have to discover a way to take the knowledge we have read and transfer it from our brain to our heart. Many people have a theological, legalistic relationship with the Lord, but He desires intimate communication and a real, heartfelt relationship with Him. People have challenges with those eighteen inches between their brain and their heart. It interrupts the true relationship our Father desires to have with us. That is why we cannot simply read the Bible and get our standard devotional time in during the day. We need to take the Word of God, meditate on it, and ponder what it means to us and how we can apply it to our lives. One of the ways I do this is to make it my prayer. If I read a love passage and want to love like that, I then cry out in desperation to the Father in prayer. I say, "God, help me to love like that!" I plea with Him to test me, try me, and help me to love His people as Christ would. If I fail the test, and occasionally I do, I get up, persevere, and seek another test until I can take what I read in the Bible and apply it to my life.

We can do the same thing with spirits that attack our mind daily. The battlefield is truly in our mind. Several times a day the enemy attempts to attack our thoughts with negativity, stress, fear, depression, or anxiety, just to name a few. We have to build up faith and believe that the Word of God says we have a "sound mind" (2 Tim. 1:7). We need to take every thought captive and make it submit to and obey the Word of God (2 Cor. 10:4-5). However, this isn't going to work for us if the information and faith are in our mind only. We need to transfer it down to our heart and make it a part of who we are. We need to walk in it, sometimes with a holy arrogance, saying, "This is my inheritance. I belong in the kingdom of love." This is not to say that we are to act in a bad, arrogant way, but we should speak and walk confidently, knowing who we are in Christ and whose we are. When you truly know that, faith becomes easy because it's in the soul, spirit, and heart of you and the essence of your very being. Faith and love are intertwined, and together they produce a remarkable spiritual result.

Jesus was seeking faith when He healed the centurion's servant:

> Now when Jesus had entered Capernaum, a centurion came to Him, pleading with Him,

saying, "Lord, my servant is lying at home paralyzed, dreadfully tormented." And Jesus said to him, "I will come and heal him." The centurion answered and said, "Lord, I am not worthy that You should come under my roof. But only speak a word, and my servant will be healed. For I also am a man under authority, having soldiers under me. And I say to this one, 'Go,' and he goes; and to another, 'Come,' and he comes; and to my servant, 'Do this,' and he does it." When Jesus heard it, He marveled, and said to those who followed, "Assuredly, I say to you, I have not found such great faith, not even in Israel! And I say to you that many will come from east and west, and sit down with Abraham, Isaac, and Jacob in the kingdom of heaven. But the sons of the kingdom will be cast out into outer darkness. There will be weeping and gnashing of teeth." Then Jesus said to the centurion, "Go your way; and as you have believed, so let it be done for you." And his servant was healed that same hour.

—MATTHEW 8:5-13

Jesus said to the man that He had not found such great faith. This man, being in faith, got Jesus to respond. When the man declared out of his mouth what he needed, Jesus immediately responded with, "I will come and heal him" (v. 7). Jesus didn't send His disciples to do the job; He was willing to do it Himself because Jesus was moved by this man's faith. I too want Jesus to be moved by my faith. I'm sure you want Jesus to be moved by your faith also.

When we proceed forward, we see in verse 13 that "Jesus said to the centurion, 'Go your way; and as you have believed, so let it be done for you.'" The centurion spoke out, pleading with him in a declaration. His words lined up with his faith. He believed, and he received. The centurion had faith because he came to Jesus. He spoke out his request. Jesus had faith. Faith was involved all around. This man took an out-spoken word and coupled it with his faith, which produced through Jesus the manifestation of his servant's healing.

Jesus said powerful words: "As you have believed" (v. 13). *Wow!* Think about that! Praise God not everything happens as we have believed, or should I say have doubted—or has it? What Job feared happened. I believe Job had a fleshly fear and fear of the Lord. However, Job's natural fear about his family, wealth, and possessions ended up happening. Our trust in the Lord must overcome any doubt or fear in the natural. But what if our belief system or doubt prevents the manifestation of our blessing? Think about that. How many things haven't happened because we got the manifestation according to our belief system? I don't like to think this can happen, and I'm sure you don't either, but the reality is that there are probably things in our lives that haven't happened yet because our faith wasn't in the proper alignment.

The centurion had such great faith that it healed his servant. A lot of us don't have faith to believe for ourselves, yet we do for another person. His faith was so great that he believed. Do you have faith to believe for yourself or others? I hope you desire giant faith that can move mountains, heal the sick, raise the dead, and cast out demons.

Knowing Scriptures and having them permeate our inner being will assist us in the realization that God desires good things to come forth in our lives. To increase in our faith we have to know it is His desire and that He will to do it. Unfortunately, the church and most of us haven't been raised in the mind-set that it is God's desire that He should bless us. We have been raised in a mentality that if we receive the smallest thing we are blessed.

God wants us to set our love upon Him, which is having a relationship with Him and to know the power and authority His name holds for us. Psalm 91 instructs us in this: "Because he has set his love upon Me, therefore I will deliver him; I will set him on high, because he has known My name. He shall call upon Me, and I will answer him; I will be with him in trouble, and I will deliver him and honor him" (Ps. 91:14-15, MEV). Knowing His name means knowing the authority of His name and the power it holds. We can't just know about Him; we must *know* Him. Searching out and memorizing Scriptures such as the ones that follow will help us to know the power of His name, His desire, and His will to do it.

> And whatever you ask in my name, that I will do, that the Father may be glorified in the Son.
>
> —JOHN 14:13

> If you ask anything in My name, I will do it.
>
> —JOHN 14:14

> If you abide in Me, and My words abide in you, you will ask what you desire, and it shall be done for you.
>
> —JOHN 15:7

> And if we know that He hears us, whatever we ask, we know that we have the petitions that we have asked of Him.
>
> —1 JOHN 5:15

To see the manifestation and line up our faith we need to abide in Him and dwell with Him. When we look at John 15:7 it says, "Abide in me." In Psalm 91 it speaks of abiding. *To abide* means to stay permanently, continue, and endure. Abiding is continuing permanently with the Lord, seeking Him, and establishing a direct relationship with Him by dwelling in the secret place of His presence.

We cannot and must not go around loosely quoting the Scriptures, thinking it will manifest goodness out of all problems. His mercy is new every morning, but His mercy is not to be abused, and neither is the Word of God. First and foremost, we need to desire Him. We should desire to know and seek a heartfelt relationship with the Father not for what He can give us, do for us, or provide for us. Not because He can turn our situation around. We should desire a relationship with Him because He created us and is our Father. If you desire a relationship with your heavenly Father, then stop right now and declare it out. Speak it!

> *Father, I desire a relationship with You. I repent. Forgive me of my sins. I accept Your Son, Jesus, as my Lord and Savior. Cleanse me, Jesus! Holy Spirit, I need You! Come upon me and fill me with the fullness and baptism of Your Spirit.*

We build our faith by being with Him, by learning about Him and what He is like. Relationships are two-way streets. And, just as you wouldn't want your kids demanding and declaring from you in a harsh voice, you don't want to speak to your Father that way. You want a loving relationship with Him, and out of that relationship you will learn what is His will to have manifested in your life. Then you can declare by faith to believe and receive your blessing or restoration. Therefore, seek God, build your faith, and discover what He has in store for you. It is greater than you can imagine!

6
SCRIPTURES WERE MEANT TO BE READ

A RE WE BLESSED to live in a day and age that we have the Bible in print and several at our disposal to read anytime, or has the written Word of God on paper enabled us to be lazy and complacent? We have been learning about the power of the out-spoken word. When I hear about the number of Christians who don't read the Word I am shocked—and yet I am not. One of my friends who I thought was a good, strong Christian with the favor of God on his life came to me for ministry. He was a successful business owner, had started a ministry, and was a leader in his church. I always admired him for his evangelistic style and being able to talk to anyone anytime about Jesus. I was shocked when he told me he hadn't read his Bible in over a year. How can a strong Christian not read their Bible?

We have any translation we desire of the Scriptures available. American believers can freely read it in public and openly talk about it for the most part, yet we fail to get in the Word every day. The Word of God was meant to be read. People want to go to church on Sunday and get their message or read a small devotional along with the scriptures that accompany it and label that as Bible reading. I think we are blessed to have a Bible we can read, but I hope more people would see it as a blessing and pick it up and read it.

Our Bibles should be read like we are studying for a college exam, but many don't read them because they don't understand what they say. Legalism has led many to believe that you can only read the original King James Version. You try to share it with other people, new believers, and people who haven't read their Bible. Often they don't understand it because of the *thee's* and *thou's*. They give up on reading or researching any other version and don't attempt to understand the written Word of God.

As we read the Bible out loud we can get more understanding, because faith comes by hearing and hearing by the Word of God. If we would pray in the spirit before reading our Bibles or pray for understanding, I am sure our Teacher, the Holy Spirit Himself, would give us the understanding we need and send confusion fleeing in the other direction.

There are many scriptures in the Bible that are statements in the form of prayers and declarations. People claim they don't know how to pray or what to pray for, but the Bible is a book full of prayer, especially the Book of Psalms. If we read the Bible out loud consistently we would be praying and studying the Scriptures at the same time and worshiping the Lord. The problem is that society has taught us to read silently in our mind and not out loud. We as parents hear teachers and educators encouraging us to read out loud to our children daily, but seldom do we do it as long as we should. Not desiring to read out loud is simply laziness, but there are so many benefits. As we read out loud, we will grow in faith, resulting in us being able to state something, like a declaration. If we read it out loud and don't understand, then we will hear that it didn't make sense. Hopefully when this happens we will stop and research it and try to understand so that no confusion remains.

Declarations will assist us in combat and warfare as we state out loud that we will not fear. They will help us to call forth the things we are waiting for. Scriptures are praise to God, and when we don't know what words to say or don't feel as if we have eloquent words we can simply recite praises to God out of the Book of Psalms. Any of the following psalms are simple statements with great power and results!

> I will not be afraid of ten thousands of people
> Who have set themselves against me all around.
> —PSALM 3:6

> I will both lie down in peace, and sleep; For You alone, O LORD, make me dwell in safety.
> —PSALM 4:8

> I will praise the LORD according to His righteousness, And will sing praise to the name of the LORD Most High.
> —PSALM 7:17

> I will be glad and rejoice in You; I will sing praise to Your name, O Most High.
> —PSALM 9:2

> I will bless the LORD who has given me counsel; My heart also instructs me in the night seasons.
> —PSALM 16:7

The LORD is my rock and my fortress and my deliverer; My God, my strength, in whom I will trust; My shield and the horn of my salvation, my stronghold.

—PSALM 18:2

I will call upon the LORD, who is worthy to be praised; So shall I be saved from my enemies.

—PSALM 18:3

Yea, though I walk through the valley of the shadow of death, I will fear no evil; For You are with me; Your rod and Your staff, they comfort me.

—PSALM 23:4

The LORD is my strength and my shield; My heart trusted in Him, and I am helped; Therefore my heart greatly rejoices, And with my song I will praise Him.

—PSALM 28:7

As for me, I will call upon God, And the LORD shall save me.

—PSALM 55:16

Whenever I am afraid, I will trust in You.

—PSALM 56:3

In God (I will praise His word), In God I have put my trust; I will not fear. What can flesh do to me?

—PSALM 56:4

In God (I will praise His word), In the Lord (I will praise His word).

—Psalm 56:10

In God I have put my trust; I will not be afraid. What can man do to me?

—Psalm 56:11

I will wait for You, O You his Strength; For God is my defense.

—Psalm 59:9

But I will sing of Your power; Yes, I will sing aloud of Your mercy in the morning; For You have been my defense And refuge in the day of my trouble.

—Psalm 59:16

I will praise the name of God with a song, And will magnify Him with thanksgiving.

—Psalm 69:30

But I will hope continually, And will praise You yet more and more.

—Psalm 71:14

I will go in the strength of the Lord God; I will make mention of Your righteousness, of Yours only.

—Psalm 71:16

Until Moses wrote the first scriptures down, the only way to convey the Word of God was through messages given from one person to another. Then, for generations, Scriptures were intended to be read aloud to others. Think about it. What if we could only receive Scripture when someone spoke it to us? I am personally thankful it's not that way and that I can read Scriptures anytime.

When we look at the Book of Psalms it is clear that they are songs. Songs were meant to be sung. The songs in the Book of Psalms were sung as affirmations on the way to the temple or on the way to war. They were sung while transitioning from one place to another. Scriptures were sung, and they still are today! If Scriptures were spoken out loud through song, then why are so many people hesitant to speak them out today? Even when Scripture is read in a church service seldom can we find a volunteer to read the scripture verse or passage out loud. It is kind of like being asked to pray out loud in front of people. No one wants to do it. It is the same with the scriptures we read. Not only do people not want to do it out loud in front of another person, but usually they don't read it out loud in their personal devotion time either, though there is power in the out-spoken word.

When we look at the Book of Psalms it is evident there are powerful praises and warfare scriptures. Look at what they were doing when speaking those warfare declarations out loud in song or word; they were sending the devil fleeing. By lifting up high the name of our Father through praise they were changing the atmosphere. Praise and worship change the atmosphere. Think about how good you feel when you speak positively or you have a joyous celebration. You feel great! We can feel great everyday, extolling and praising the name of our Father through Scripture!

Warfare hits us at unexpected times, and often we don't know how we should pray. Vengeance is God's, not ours. The best we can sometimes do in these situations is to quote the spiritual warfare psalms out loud in a desperate plea to our Father.

> In my distress, I cried to the LORD, And He heard me. Deliver my soul, O LORD, from lying lips And from a deceitful tongue. What shall be given to you, Or what shall be done to you, You false tongue? Sharp arrows of the warrior, With coals of the broom tree! Woe is me, that I dwell in Meshech, That I dwell among the tents of Kedar! My soul has dwelt too long with one who hates peace. I am for peace; But when I speak, they are for war.
>
> —PSALM 120:1-7

When you speak out psalms in warfare declaration you are speaking out the purest form of prayer. When we are upset with one another we are tempted to pray out of the soul, out of our own fleshy ambitions and will, or to pray manipulative prayers that are for our benefit or retribution instead of seeking the Holy Spirit to convict them. By praying the psalms we are praying according to God's Word and allowing Him to be the vindicator.

> LORD, how they have increased who trouble me! Many are they who rise up against me. Many are they who say of me, "There is no help for him in God." Selah. But You, O LORD, are a shield for me, My glory and the One who lifts up my head. I cried to the LORD with my voice, And He heard me from His holy hill. Selah. I lay down and slept; I awoke, for the LORD sustained me. I will not be afraid of ten thousands of people Who have set themselves against me all around. Arise, O LORD; Save me,

O my God! For You have struck all my enemies
on the cheekbone; You have broken the teeth
of the ungodly. Salvation belongs to the LORD.
Your blessing is upon Your people. Selah

—PSALM 3:1-8

When we look at the songs of ascent we see that they
are declarations, statements of who God is and what you
want Him to be for you. They are personal and intimate.
There is an assurance in them of God's protective hand
upon you, and it is comforting. Again, reading these out
loud at any time will benefit your spirit and soul.

I will lift up my eyes to the hills—From whence
comes my help? My help comes from the LORD,
Who made heaven and earth. He will not allow
your foot to be moved; He who keeps you will
not slumber. Behold, He who keeps Israel Shall
neither slumber nor sleep. The LORD is your
keeper; The LORD is your shade at your right
hand. The sun shall not strike you by day, Nor
the moon by night. The LORD shall preserve
you from all evil; He shall preserve your soul.
The LORD shall preserve your going out and
your coming in From this time forth, and
even forevermore.

—PSALM 121:1-8

Psalms are praises and reasons to celebrate. It is
challenging for a lot of people to come up with the words
to praise the Lord. We have been raised to give God
our grocery list of problems and challenges and not to
praise Him with our lips, but in Psalm 100 we are given
instructions on how to enter into our time with the
Lord: "Enter into His gates with thanksgiving, And into

His courts with praise. Be thankful to Him, and bless His name" (Ps. 100:4). God doesn't only want to hear our grocery list or prayer list when we go into our secret place or prayer and worship time with Him. God desires us to "enter into His gates with thanksgiving, And into His courts with praise" (v. 4). We find it easy to thank Him for the natural things, like food, health, and provision, because these blessings come to our mind easily, but too often we find ourselves running out of thankful words and end our time of thanksgiving before we should. When we have finished expressing thanks for them we enter into our prayer time, ask for our needs, and start our worship time without ever truly entering into His presence. How do we enter into His gates with thanksgiving?

Looking at Psalm 100:4, we discover that He wants us to enter in with thanksgiving. Thanksgiving is giving an expression of gratitude to God. What are you thankful for? I remember my mother-in-law was always thankful for all of the different shades of green and all of the different kinds of trees. When you think of God's creativity there is plenty to be thankful for.

By releasing some prayers of thanksgiving from our lips we can focus our mind, attitude, and spirit on the living God. Focus your attention and affections on the One you love and are praying to and worshiping. When approaching your secret place, take a moment and simply breathe. Breathe in the presence of God. Then, as you focus and settle down, speak out words of thanksgiving to Him. Don't try to think about what you are thankful for; you don't want to get your mind going. You are trying to get your mind settled down so you can enter into the presence of God.

You could start your prayer time with some of these thoughts:

I bless You, Lord.

I thank You for this day.

Marvelous are the works of Your hands.

How great are Your ways.

You've searched me and know me.

I open up my heart to You.

Favor is my portion.

I exalt You, Lord.

I lift Your name up high.

How magnificent is Your name.

I love You, Lord.

Think about how our prayer and worship time could change and be elevated if we would start by words of affirmation to our Father before praying and worshiping. Speaking out words to our Father will help us still our heart and soul before the Father so that we can connect with Him spirit to Spirit.

We tend to lead busy and hurried lives, and then we expect to all of a sudden sit down and pray or stand up and sing when there are so many other things running through our mind. One of the main things Christians can complain about is that they can't hear from God. When we settle ourselves down, enter in with thanksgiving, and speak words of praise, we will hear from God. We have stilled ourselves and put ourselves in a posture of receiving.

Try starting your prayer and praise time differently, with thanksgiving, and discover how it will enhance and increase the rest of your spiritual life. God longs to hear from you, and His ears are open to you. Open your mouth now, and speak praises to His ears. Bless His holy name! If you still discover you can't find the right words to praise the Lord, then read a psalm such as the one below or one of the many other psalms of praise.

> It is good to give thanks to the LORD, And to sing praises to Your name, O Most High; To declare Your lovingkindness in the morning, And Your faithfulness every night, On an instrument of ten strings, On the lute, And on the harp, With harmonious sound. For You, LORD, have made me glad through Your work; I will triumph in the works of Your hands. O LORD, how great are Your works! Your thoughts are very deep. A senseless man does not know, Nor does a fool understand this. When the wicked spring up like grass, And when all the workers of iniquity flourish, It is that they may be destroyed forever. But You, LORD, are on high forevermore. For behold, Your enemies, O LORD, For behold, Your enemies shall perish; All the workers of iniquity shall be scattered. But my horn You have exalted like a wild ox; I have been anointed with fresh oil. My eye also has seen my desire on my enemies; My ears hear my desire on the wicked Who rise up against me. The righteous

shall flourish like a palm tree, He shall grow like a cedar in Lebanon. Those who are planted in the house of the LORD Shall flourish in the courts of our God. They shall still bear fruit in old age; They shall be fresh and flourishing, To declare that the LORD is upright; He is my rock, and there is no unrighteousness in Him.

—PSALM 92:1-15

As we start reading the Scriptures differently and pay attention to filler words we will discover that there is more to discover. I've said it many times before, yet I will say it again: The filler words are important. They connect the dots, so to speak. Pay attention to the filler word *read* in this passage: "Now when this epistle is read among you, see that it is also read in the church of the Laodiceans, and that you likewise read the epistle from Laodicea" (Col. 4:16). We are instructed in the Scriptures to read the epistle, read the letters, or we are told that they went to the tabernacle and something was read. The Scriptures show the importance of reading, saying, or declaring out loud the written Word, some of which is prayer and worship.

And he took the Book of the Covenant and read in the audience of the people. And they said, "All that the LORD has said will we do, and be obedient."

—EXODUS 24:7

And it shall be with him, and he shall read it all the days of his life, that he may learn to fear the LORD his God and be careful to observe all the words of this law and these statutes.

—DEUTERONOMY 17:19

When all Israel comes to appear before the
LORD your God in the place which He chooses,
you shall read this law before all Israel in
their hearing.

—DEUTERONOMY 31:11

And afterward he read all the words of the law,
the blessings and the cursings, according to all
that is written in the Book of the Law. There was
not a word of all that Moses commanded which
Joshua did not read before all the assembly of
Israel, with the women, the little ones, and the
strangers who were living among them.

—JOSHUA 8:34-35

And Hezekiah received the letter from the hand
of the messengers, and read it; and Hezekiah
went up to the house of the LORD, and spread it
before the LORD.

—2 KINGS 19:14

Then Hilkiah the high priest said unto Shaphan
the scribe, "I have found the Book of the Law
in the house of the LORD." And Hilkiah gave
the book to Shaphan, and he read it.... Then
Shaphan the scribe shewed the king, saying,
"Hilkiah the priest has given me a book." And
Shaphan read it before the king.

—2 KINGS 22:8, 10

And the king went up to the house of the LORD
with all the men of Judah, and with him all
the inhabitants of Jerusalem—the priests and
the prophets and all the people, both small
and great. And he read in their hearing all the

words of the Book of the Covenant which was found in the house of the LORD.

—2 KINGS 23:2

Then Shaphan the scribe told the king, saying, "Hilkiah the priest has given me a book." And Shaphan read it before the king.

—2 CHRONICLES 34:18

The king went up into the house of the LORD, with all the men of Judah and the inhabitants of Jerusalem—the priests and the Levites, and all the people, great and small. And he read in their hearing all the words of the Book of the Covenant which had been found in the house of the LORD.

—2 CHRONICLES 34:30

So they read distinctly from the book, in the Law of God; and they gave the sense, and helped them to understand the reading.

—NEHEMIAH 8:8

Also day by day, from the first day until the last day, he read from the Book of the Law of God. And they kept the feast seven days; and on the eighth day there was a sacred assembly, according to the prescribed manner.

—NEHEMIAH 8:18

And they stood up in their place and read from the Book of the Law of the LORD their God one-fourth part of the day; and for another fourth they confessed and worshiped the LORD their God.

—NEHEMIAH 9:3

On that day they read from the Book of Moses in the hearing of the people, and in it was found written that the Ammonite or Moabite should ever come into the assembly of God.

—NEHEMIAH 13:1

Search from the book of the LORD, and read: Not one of these shall fail; Not one shall lack her mate. For my mouth has commanded it, and His Spirit has gathered them.

—ISAIAH 34:16

You go, therefore, and read from the scroll which you have written at my instruction, the words of the LORD, in the hearing of the people in the LORD's house on the day of fasting. And you shall also read them in the hearing of all Judah who come from their cities.

—JEREMIAH 36:6

And they said to him, "Sit down now, and read it in our hearing." So Baruch read it in their hearing.

—JEREMIAH 36:15

So He came to Nazareth, where he had been brought up. And as His custom was, He went into the synagogue on the Sabbath day, and stood up to read.

—LUKE 4:16

For those who dwell in Jerusalem, and their rulers, because they did not know Him, nor even the voices of the Prophets which are read every Sabbath, have fulfilled them in condemning Him.

—ACTS 13:27

For Moses has had throughout many generations those who preach him in every city, being read in the synagogues every Sabbath.

—ACTS 15:21

Now when this epistle is read among you, see that it is read also in the church of the Laodiceans, and that you likewise read the epistle from Laodicea.

—COLOSSIANS 4:16

I charge you by the Lord that this epistle be read to all the holy brethren.

—1 THESSALONIANS 5:27

We must be reading the written Word out loud, just as we read books to our children. As we do, our children learn and grow. We have all read Dr. Seuss's *Green Eggs and Ham*, and we have recited, "I do not like them, Sam–I–am."[1] Those words don't have power and authority, as the Word of God does. However, they show us that if we hear something enough we will repeat it. We don't always know Scripture by memory, but for those of us who attended vacation Bible school and had to memorize a scripture for one week, we still know the scripture and the reference. I know, because at one of the schools my son had to memorize a verse, and it became his favorite Bible verse.

Think about how much more knowledge and how much better versed in the Word of God we could be if we heard the Scriptures more frequently. For some of us nightly Bible reading at the dinner table has become routine, but it often doesn't go past those few minutes at supper time. Imagine how your family's understanding of the Scriptures would increase with a few extra minutes of reading the Word aloud. My husband has a Bible by his bedside, and there are times in the night and morning when he will pick it up and read it to me. I so enjoy, even at my age and place in life, having the Word of God read and spoken over my life.

Try something different. Perhaps it won't be all the time, but try reading more frequently than you have before, and discover the benefits you will reap.

7
LORD, YOU
SAID IF I ASK

GOD INSTRUCTS US in His Word to ask of Him. When we think of declaring it really is putting a demand on the spiritual realm. People do not always understand that we can put a demand on God to bring something forth in our life. He instructs us to ask, so why aren't we asking? Religion has taught us to respect God, to be quiet and submit. We can be both respectful and submissive in the process of inquiring.

As we pray to God we may receive revelation back into our soul and spirit. When we get this revelation often we act on it without considering it any further. What we have to realize when we hear from God is that our own thoughts, our imaginations, and the enemy can send confusion into our thinking. What if we thought we heard from God and it was really a different source that we heard from? (I explain this more in my book, *Flesh, Satan, or God: Who Are You Hearing From?*) Since people get confused in hearing we should inquire of the Father to discern if the instruction we are hearing is truly from Him. We can test the spirits or the Scriptures to see if what we are receiving is lining up with the Word of God and in accordance with the direction we think God would give.

People think it is disrespectful to question God. We aren't being disrespectful. We are making sure we aren't looking to the left or right and are staying on the path that our heavenly Father has laid out for us, not getting sidetracked along the way. Our imagination is a wild thing. Our flesh can get involved with our own ideas, and the enemy can send confusion into the equation in order to prevent you from following God's path. Inquiring of God to get the discernment you need will assist you in declaring for the revelation that He has given you.

Changing our mentality to believe that it is alright to inquire of the Lord and declare things according to His will is in alignment with Matthew 7:7: "Ask, and it will be given to you; seek, and you will find; knock, and it will be opened to you." *Ask* is an action word. People quote the following verse loosely, yet there is truth to it: "You do not have because you do not ask" (James 4:2). Asking involves opening our mouth and putting our faith to action. Instead of sitting around, waiting to see if God will give us something or change our situation, why don't we pray and call forth the manifestation of our blessing or declare for our situation to change? He isn't going to drop something simply out of the sky. He desires to hear His children communicate with Him.

We cannot sit silent and passive and always wait for the Lord to unction us in the spirit. In the Bible we read that people went to inquire of the Lord.

> But the children struggled together within her;
> and she said, "If all is well, why am I like this?"
> So she went to inquire of the LORD.
>
> —GENESIS 25:22

> So they said to him, "Please inquire of God, that
> we may know whether the journey on which we
> go will be prosperous."
>
> —JUDGES 18:5

When we look at these scriptures we see that they questioned God. Many of us would not dare question God; we would take our prayer revelation at face value. Did you ever stop to think that perhaps God was going to add additional instructions, but you left your prayer closet too early, and by going back to inquire of Him you would have received information pertinent to the direction He gave you? Of course, we don't think that way. We assume that God is done speaking to us at that moment. What if you need to digest what He has given you before He can reveal more? What if you don't realize that you got distracted or interrupted, or your flesh was tired of praying or sitting there and you got up before it was time? God doesn't always speak continuously. He will speak to us, allow us to process or write it down, even allowing us time to absorb it, and then He can speak to us again. When you are seeking revelation and direction you need to pause and always wait and inquire and see if there is more.

In Malachi 3 we see a good example that we can relate to about inquiring of God.

> "Bring all the tithes into the storehouse, That
> there may be food in My house, And try Me

now in this," Says the Lord of hosts, "If I will not open for you the windows of heaven And pour out for you such blessing That there will not be room enough to receive it. And I will rebuke the devourer for your sakes, So that he will not destroy the fruit of your ground, Nor shall the vine fail to bear fruit for you in the field," Says the Lord of hosts.

—Malachi 3:10-11

In these verses God is inviting us to try Him in this. Here He is allowing us to engage in what some people would call challenging God. He is saying, "Try Me; try to prove Me wrong, because you can't." In essence, He is inviting us to question Him, inquire of Him, and see if He is speaking the truth to us—and He is! I've seen God bless! If we can try Him in this why can't we inquire of Him?

God also instructs us in His Word to remind Him of His Word. This is another area that is extremely useful in declaring. He says, "Put Me in remembrance; Let us contend together; State your case, that you may be acquitted" (Isa. 43:26). Put Him in remembrance, and remind Him of what you did and His Word.

In His Word there are several places where we see the phrase "Remember, Lord":

Remember, O Lord, Your tender mercies and Your loving kindnesses, For they are from of old.

—Psalm 25:6

Remember, Lord, the reproach of Your servants— How I bear in my bosom the reproach of all the many peoples.

—Psalm 89:50

> Remember now, O Lord, how I have walked
> before You in truth and with a loyal heart, and
> have done what is good in Your sight.
>
> —Isaiah 38:3

One way of reminding the Lord and calling forth is through His Word. By reading and quoting the above scriptures and much more throughout the Bible you can remind God of His Word.

When we study the Word, it is full of actions that need to be taken on our part that are connected to results and conditions. There are things we have to do to get what the Word says. When we look at Psalm 91 we can see that there is something we need to do.

> He who dwells in the secret place of the
> Most High Shall abide under the shadow of
> the Almighty.
>
> —Psalm 91:1

There is a condition in the beginning of this verse with the results appearing at the end of the verse. You have to dwell in the secret place in order to abide. You have something to do in order to get the result. The word *dwell* means "to establish, inhabit,"[1] as well as "take up homestead, stake out a claim, possess a place, and live within."[2] When we look at the definition of *dwell* we see that it is filled with action words and responsibility. There is a condition: When you do this, then you will receive the protection of the shadow of the Almighty. Abiding is the result of our dwelling. To abide is to "stay permanently, endure," and "tarry."[3] I think we can all agree that we would like that from our heavenly Father. All we have to do is dwell. And

I don't know about you, but I love dwelling with Him and being in His presence.

The word *he* in verse 1 is representative of an individual person. We need to make sure that we are not only dwelling corporately but privately in that secret hiding place. That means communion, intimate fellowship, and relationship with God. It is being in that place of solitude and rest so that we can rightfully declare out what He is depositing. When we dwell He will then protect. When we dwell we have a right to make a demand on God's Word through declaring for Him to protect us.

As we go further into this passage we continue to see that God protects us, but then He reminds us again of what we have to do:

> I will say of the Lord, "He is my refuge and my fortress; My God, in Him I will trust." Surely He shall deliver you from the snare of the fowler And from the perilous pestilence. He shall cover you with His feathers, And under His wings you shall take refuge; His truth shall be your shield and buckler. You shall not be afraid of the terror by night, Nor of the arrow that flies by day, Nor of the pestilence that walks in darkness, Nor of the destruction that lays waste at noonday. A thousand may fall at your side, And ten thousand at your right hand; But it shall not come near you. Only with your eyes shall you look, And see the reward of the wicked.
>
> —PSALM 91:2-8

He is a God we can trust. We can flee to Him for protection. He is our shelter. I love the analogy of the eagle's wing, and I just think about being wrapped up in

His big, soft, feathery, strong wing. In *The Message* Bible it says, "I trust in you, and I'm safe." That is a declaration and one that we all need to make as we struggle with trust. When we study these verses we learn that He delivers us from the demonic realm, hidden traps, infection, sickness, and plagues! That is the kind of covering we need! *To cover* means "to entwine, fence in, cover over, and protect."[4] I enjoy the analogy of being fenced in by God.

What I want you to notice in verse 2 is the word *say*. It says, "I will say of the LORD." The word *say* refers to an out-loud declaration. David is declaring out loud, verbally, with his voice. He is not thinking in his mind but stating outwardly.

When we dwell with Him and close ourselves in with Him, He closes Himself in with us. That is just like our Father, because He loves us so much! He is our shield and buckler (v. 4), protecting our body, the vital parts, against the weapons and arrows of the enemy. People wonder why some get spiritual attacks and others don't. The answer has everything to do with the importance of dwelling. Some people put in the time to be with Him, and some just expect His protection no matter what they do. We shall not be afraid of evil, but evil can manifest in several ways, which includes but is not limited to betrayal, robbery, and murder.

The word *surely* in verse 3 is declaring that something is going to happen. Therefore, when we dwell and abide we are experiencing a declaration of fact that "surely He shall deliver you from the snare of the fowler."

In verses 4-6, David continues to tell us about our protection. However, when we study these verses, especially verse 5, He is instructing us to pray offensively. We need to be prophetically speaking and declaring life and prophesying over ourselves what the Lord is going to do and how He is going to protect us (v. 7). The Word in verse 5 is telling us, "You shall not be afraid." It is declaring a fact over you that you should be declaring over yourself: "I shall not be afraid."

Studying this out, God not only keeps us from evil but the fear of evil. When we bring alongside 2 Timothy 1:7—"For God has not given us a spirit of fear, but of power and of love and of a sound mind"—we have another declaration. We have a sound mind. That means we shall not fear, and we have to be declaring out, calling into existence what we already have.

God continues to protect us in verses 6 and 7, declaring over us that when people are dying on all sides of us we are not to be afraid. In the days in which we are living we see natural disasters, terrorists, and diseases. Through David, God is prophetically declaring His promise to protect and keep you in spite of the chaos in the world.

In verse 9 God reminds us again about making Him our dwelling place: "Because you have made the LORD, who is my refuge, Even the Most High, your dwelling place." The term *dwelling place* means "habitation." We don't want a visitation from the Father or Jesus, like so many people for years have been crying out for. We want habitation, which is permanent residency. *Visitation* means that He is going to come and go. We want to reside permanently with Him and dwell with Him at all times. Again, David is prophesying over you the fact of what you should be doing, which is being in the Lord's presence.

> No evil shall befall you, Nor shall any plague come near your dwelling; For He shall give His angels charge over you, To keep you in all your

ways. In their hands they shall bear you up, Lest
you dash your foot against a stone. You shall
tread upon the lion and the cobra, The young
lion and the serpent you shall trample underfoot.

—Psalm 91:10-13

God keeps us from pestilence, sickness, and destruction.
When people are dying on all sides of you it shall not come
near you! That is reason alone not to worry or fear. How
many times have you worried about bird flu, Ebola, AIDS,
or salmonella when you heard about them or have been
exposed to them? Don't fear in the midst of a terrorist
attack. Just repeatedly tell yourself, "He is my shelter, my
strength. In Him I will trust." Don't worry or fear. He will
protect you! We will have spiritual authority over satanic
powers; nothing shall harm us!

David ends the psalm by reminding us to again dwell
with God, but this time it is because we love Him, have a
relationship with Him, and know Him.

Because he has set his love upon Me, therefore I
will deliver him; I will set him on high, because
he has known My name. He shall call upon
Me, and I will answer him; I will be with him
in trouble; I will deliver him and honor him.
With long life I will satisfy him, And show
him My salvation.

—Psalm 91:14-16

In the Book of John it also talks of abiding in Him: "If
you abide in Me, and My words abide in you, you will ask
what you desire, and it shall be done for you" (John 15:7).
Here we are encouraged not only to abide but also to ask
for what we desire. He is a Father who loves to give to us.

> If you then, being evil, know how to give good gifts to your children, how much more will your Father who is in heaven give good things to those who ask Him!
>
> —Matthew 7:11

When asking God and calling forth a declaration the first thing you need to do is make sure it is in accordance with His will.

> Now this is the confidence that we have in Him, that if we ask anything according to His will, He hears us. And if we know that He hears us, whatever we ask, we know that we have the petitions that we have asked of Him.
>
> —1 John 5:14-15

Declaring is not for everything we want. If it were, everyone would have everything and would go around declaring all the time. The Scriptures give us the guideline for declaring by saying, "In accordance to His will." He will reveal His will to you and guide you in declaring by His Spirit.

In declaring, you need to believe that you will receive: "And whatever things you ask in prayer, believing, you will receive" (Matt. 21:22). You don't want to declare and not align your faith with it. James tells us to ask in faith: "But let him ask in faith, with no doubting, for he who doubts is like a wave of the sea driven and tossed by the wind" (James 1:6).

When declaring, ask in the name of Jesus according to John 14:13-14: "And whatever you ask in My name, that I will do, that the Father may be glorified in the Son. If you ask anything in My name, I will do it." Ask in the name of

Jesus! When I declare and decree, at the end of the entire declaration or each sentence, depending on what I am declaring for, I say, "In the name of Jesus." In order to ask in the name of Jesus you need to know there is power in the name of Jesus. When we study God's Word it teaches us about the spoken Word of God. It talks about what we say. It is the words we speak out that are powerful! The strongest word that we can speak out is the name of Jesus. One word. One name—the name of our Lord and Savior.

Proverbs 18:10 tells us, "The name of the LORD is a strong tower; the righteous run to it and are safe." The name of Jesus saves, not just as our Deliverer and Redeemer but as our Protector (Ps. 91). I love studying from the Complete Jewish Bible. I read that translation and love it for this verse. Proverbs 18:10 in the Complete Jewish Bible reads, "The name of ADONAI is a strong tower; a righteous person runs to it and is raised high [above danger]." The name of Jesus does raise us high above danger when we call it out!

The name of Jesus heals, sets free, saves, delivers, and much more. The name of Jesus can cast out a demon. It can take an evil spirit that has invaded someone's life, and by the name of Jesus that spirit has to disembody the person! That is a miracle to be able to cast out a demon from a person. That is the power of Jesus' name. The power of His name creates miracles.

In order to run to Jesus for protection and use His name appropriately we have to know that we know the power of that name. We must saturate ourselves with stories and testimonies of the power of His name. We must read books on our identity in Christ and how He died and descended to hell for us and then on the third day ascended to heaven. We need to know that He transferred His power of attorney to us. That's right. His Word says in Luke 10:19, "Behold, I give you authority to trample on serpents and scorpions, and over all the power of the enemy, and nothing shall by any means hurt you."

Knowing the name of Jesus, the power and authority it holds, and how we are to use it, comes from knowing our identity in Christ. We must know our identity in Christ. You must know who you are in Christ—that you are valuable, that you are of the kingdom, that you are from a world that cannot be shaken. In Acts 2:25 it says, "For David says concerning Him: 'I foresaw the Lord always before my face, For He is at my right hand, that I may not be shaken.'" We must know the name and power of Jesus.

What you are decreeing for according to God's will is already loosed in heaven. There is a natural and spiritual correlation. We need to speak out with faith what it is and loose it with our words on Earth.

> Assuredly, I say to you, whatever you bind on earth will be bound in heaven, and whatever you loose on earth will be loosed in heaven.
>
> —Matthew 18:18

> Yes! I tell you people that whatever you prohibit on earth will be prohibited in heaven, and whatever you permit on earth will be permitted in heaven.
>
> —Matthew 18:18, cjb

> I promise you that God in heaven will allow whatever you allow on earth, but he will not allow anything you don't allow.
>
> —Matthew 18:18, cev

> Truly I tell you, whatever you forbid and declare to be improper and unlawful on earth

must be what is already forbidden in heaven, and whatever you permit and declare proper and lawful on earth must be what is already permitted in heaven.

—Matthew 18:18, ampc

As we look at these verses on binding and loosing we see that it is a choice, our choice, what we are going to bind and loose on Earth and in heaven. It is so important that we speak out, that we declare. The power is in our hands. God is giving us free choice. He is giving us the tools to destroy the power of the enemy and loose things on this earth that we need in order to have a victorious, successful life.

Are you going to sit around and do nothing if someone gives you the keys to open a lock and receive everything inside? We have heaven co-laboring with us and at our disposal, yet still we choose to keep silent instead of speaking out against our circumstances. We have to move past the victim mentality that it is someone else's responsibility to change our situation and realize that it is our responsibility. We can change our situation by speaking because He hears our prayers, and He is open and attentive to us.

And I said: "I pray, Lord God of heaven, O great and awesome God, You who keep Your covenant and mercy with those who love You and observe Your commandments, please let Your ear be attentive and Your eyes open, that You may hear the prayer of Your servant which I pray before You now, day and night, for the children of Israel Your servants, and confess the sins of the children of Israel which we have

SPEAK OUT

sinned against You. Both my father's house and
I have sinned."

—NEHEMIAH 1:5-6

Nehemiah, when praying for His people, *said*. In verse
five it says, "I said." Nehemiah was petitioning out loud,
verbally, for the people. But he didn't just *say*. When we
look at this verse in full context, it says, "I said," and, "I
pray." The words *say* and *pray* are in the same verse. Here
we see a correlation between saying and praying with
Nehemiah saying his prayer.

Nehemiah is petitioning to God for His ear to be
attentive. He is petitioning God to hear and listen to the
prayer of His servant. Nehemiah is petitioning God to
hear him, indicating that it was a verbal prayer. Otherwise,
why would he be correlating saying, praying, and hearing
all in the same passage?

As we abide in the Lord we will know the power of the
name of Jesus. God's Word says, "Therefore submit to
God. Resist the devil and he will flee from you. Draw near
to God and He will draw near to you" (James 4:7-8). By
being with God in His presence and obeying His Word we
are submitting to God and closing the entry points to the
devil in our lives. As we bind and loose in faith we glorify
His name and get the assistance we need. He promises,
"Call upon Me in the day of trouble; I will deliver you, and
you shall glorify Me" (Ps. 50:15).

When He assists us and we speak out His Word, then
"'no weapon formed against you shall prosper, And every
tongue which rises against you in judgment You shall
condemn. This is the heritage of the servants of the LORD,
And their righteousness is from Me,' Says the LORD"
(Isa. 54:17). When we are in right standing with God this

is our portion, our inheritance. However, we also have to renew our mind, get rid of legalism, and know our identity and authority so that we can understand, believe, and receive the inheritance that is ours through Christ Jesus.

Our inheritance is for God to bless us.

> Now it shall come to pass, if you diligently obey the voice of the LORD your God, to observe carefully all His commandments which I command you today, that the LORD your God will set you high above all nations of the earth. And all these blessings shall come upon you and overtake you, because you obey the voice of the LORD your God: Blessed shall you be in the city, and blessed shall you be in the country. Blessed shall be the fruit of your body, the produce of your ground and the increase of your herds, the increase of your cattle and the offspring of your flocks. Blessed shall be your basket and your kneading bowl. Blessed shall you be when you come in, and blessed shall you be when you go out. The LORD will cause your enemies who rise against you to be defeated before your face; they shall come out against you one way and flee before you seven ways. The LORD will command the blessing on you in your storehouses and in all to which you set your hand, and He will bless you in the land which the LORD your God is giving you. The LORD will establish you as a holy people to Himself, just as He has sworn to you, if you keep the commandments of the LORD your God and walk in His ways. Then all peoples of the earth shall see that you are called by the name of the LORD, and they shall be afraid of you. And the LORD will grant you

plenty of goods, in the fruit of your body, in the increase of your livestock, and in the produce of your ground, in the land of which the LORD swore to your fathers to give you. The LORD will open to you His good treasure, the heavens, to give the rain to your land in its season, and to bless all the work of your hand. You shall lend to many nations, but you shall not borrow. And the LORD will make you the head and not the tail; you shall be above only, and not be beneath if you heed the commandments of the LORD your God, which I command you today, and are careful to observe them.

—DEUTERONOMY 28:1-13

Our God is not a God who wants us to live in a menial way. He desires to bless us and bless us in abundance. The Word empowers you, but that empowerment won't become real to you if you don't know the entitlement the Word says you can have. His Word tells us to remind Him of what we can have. In Deuteronomy God lists out how He will bless us, but we also find other scriptures where we are told that if we do this, He will do that. And He wants us to remind Him.

In Jeremiah God says that when we call upon Him He will listen, and when we seek Him we will find Him.

Then you will call upon Me and go and pray to Me, and I will listen to you. And you will seek Me and find Me, when you search for Me with all your heart.

—JEREMIAH 29:12-13

The way I would encourage you to remind Him is by saying out loud the following in your prayer time:

God, Your Word says that You will listen to me when I call upon You. Now I have called upon You and prayed to You. Consider and listen to my petitions. You said in Your Word that I would seek You and find You. Lord, I have searched for You with all my heart. I have prayed, worshiped, and spent time in solitude. Lord, I want to know You even more than I already do.

In these instances we are reminding God with love, intimacy, fellowship, and desire in order to get to know Him better. We aren't being crass or disrespectful. We are reminding Him of the fellowship that He too desires with us. We are asking Him to listen to our petitions and pleas out of adoration for who He is, knowing that He can provide all our needs.

We can inquire of the Father about His Word and about prospering in our ways.

> This Book of the Law shall not depart from your mouth, but you shall meditate in it day and night, that you may observe to do according to all that is written in it. For then you will make your way prosperous, and then you will have good success.
>
> —JOSHUA 1:8

God, Your Word says to meditate on Your Word. I have studied Your Word and meditated on it. You say that I will prosper in all my ways and have good success. I call that prosperity and success forth in the mighty name of Jesus, Yeshua Messiah!

He also removes our sins as far as the east is from the west: "As far as the east is from the west, So far has He removed our transgressions from us" (Ps. 103:12).

> Lord, Your written Word says, "I, even I, am He who blots out your transgressions for My own sake; And I will not remember your sins" (Isa. 43:25). Lord, please forgive me of all my sins, all of my inadequacies, and when I entertain thoughts in my mind that are not of You. Forgive me when I act out in the behaviors of anger, rejection, or control. Lord, remember that You will remove my transgressions and blot out my sins and remember them no more.

Make your declarations and remembrances personal. Find a situation and scripture that has happened to you, and call forth the blessing from the trial or tragedy.

> And everyone who has left houses or brothers or sisters or father or mother or wife or children or lands, for My name's sake, shall receive a hundredfold, and inherit eternal life.
> —MATTHEW 19:29

My husband and I have given up our home several times for the sake of the kingdom, and it did cause some damage in relationships. Therefore, this is personal to me. So I would say, "Lord, remember when we gave up family or homes for Your name. Your Word says that I will receive a hundredfold, and I shall inherit eternal life."

Now, I don't believe that the references to a hundredfold and prosperity are always about money. I would rather be rich in spiritual knowledge than anything else any day. Therefore, don't always look for a financial payback. Sometimes it comes in elevation, a deeper anointing, and blessings in buying things inexpensively. After all, that is money in our pockets. Just claim and call forth the blessing you are entitled to and allow God to do the rest.

I remind Him of His Word when it comes to ministry. After all, why wouldn't it be according to God's will for me to have ministry expansion as long as I am living righteously and glorifying His name?

> And whoever will not receive you, when you go out of that city, shake off the very dust from your feet as a testimony against them.
>
> —LUKE 9:5

Once my husband and I literally parked our vehicle and left the kids in the van for a brief moment while we stepped right outside the vehicle and shook the dust off from our feet. Now I pray, "Lord, remember the cities and regions I left at your instruction and when I shook the dust off my feet. Remember, Lord, the ministry connections I broke and severed that were tied to Jezebel spirits. I was obedient to your instruction and Word, Lord. Now, remember and expand my territory. I call forth more regions and territories and more churches and ministries that will receive me and the prophetic teachings You desire to impart into those places.

> *Father, even Your Son, Jesus, was not welcome in His own town: "Then He said, 'Assuredly, I say to you, no prophet is accepted in his own country'" (Luke 4:24). Lord, remember that we are not always welcome in our hometown. Send me where I will have honor and where the word*

*I speak will be heard and received. I call forth
new divine appointments where I can impart
the Holy Spirit's wisdom and revelation.*

We can prosper when we are obedient to Him. First
Kings 2:3 instructs us, "And keep the charge of the Lord
your God; to walk in His ways, to keep His statutes, His
commandments, His judgments, and His testimonies, as it
is written in the Law of Moses, that you may prosper in all
that you do and wherever you turn."

*Lord, thank You that I have walked in Your
ways. I call forth the manifestation that I will
prosper in all I do and wherever I turn.*

Call forth and declare and remind the Lord of the life
you have lived to serve Him well or the life your parent or
grandparent lived that was sold out to the Lord. Use that to
call forth the heritage of your children and to bring in the
lost family members, according to Leviticus 26:45: "But for
their sake I will remember the covenant of their ancestors,
whom I brought out of the land of Egypt in the sight of
the nations, that I might be their God: I am the Lord."

*It is written, Lord, that You will remember the
covenant of my ancestors. I call forth that You
will be the Lord God of my family and children.*

One of the best ways to inquire of the Father is by
blessing Him and calling forth things that are going to
assist us in our spiritual walk.

Oh, that my ways were directed To keep
Your statutes!

—Psalm 119:5

Then I would not be ashamed, When I look into all Your commandments.

—Psalm 119:6

I will praise You with uprightness of heart, When I learn Your righteous judgments.

—Psalm 119:7

With my whole heart I have sought You; Oh, let me not wander from Your commandments!

—Psalm 119:10

Your word I have hidden in my heart, That I might not sin against You!

—Psalm 119:11

Blessed are You, O Lord! Teach me Your statutes.

—Psalm 119:12

I will meditate on Your precepts, And contemplate Your ways.

—Psalm 119:15

I will delight myself in Your statutes; I will not forget Your word.

—Psalm 119:16

Deal bountifully with Your servant, That I may live and keep Your word.

—Psalm 119:17

Open my eyes, that I may see Wondrous things from Your law.

—Psalm 119:18

I have declared my ways, and You answered me;
Teach me Your statutes.

—Psalm 119:26

Make me understand the way of Your precepts;
So shall I meditate on Your wonderful works.

—Psalm 119:27

Give me understanding, and I shall keep Your
law; Indeed, I shall observe it with my whole
heart.

—Psalm 119:34

Remember the word to Your servant, Upon which
You have caused me to hope.

—Psalm 119:49

You are my portion, O Lord; I have said that I
would keep Your words.

—Psalm 119:57

I entreated Your favor with my whole heart; Be
merciful to me according to Your word.

—Psalm 119:58

Let my heart be blameless regarding Your statutes,
That I may not be ashamed.

—Psalm 119:80

Forever, O Lord, Your word is settled in heaven.

—Psalm 119:89

Your faithfulness endures to all generations;
You established the earth, and it abides.

—Psalm 119:90

I am Yours, save me; For I have sought Your precepts.

—Psalm 119:94

Oh, how I love Your law! It is my meditation all the day.

—Psalm 119:97

You, through Your commandments, make me wiser than my enemies; For they are ever with me.

—Psalm 119:98

Your word is a lamp to my feet And a light to my path.

—Psalm 119:105

My life is continually in my hand, Yet I do not forget Your law.

—Psalm 119:109

You are my hiding place and my shield; I hope in Your word.

—Psalm 119:114

Hold me up, and I shall be safe, And I shall observe Your statutes continually.

—Psalm 119:117

Your testimonies are wonderful; Therefore my soul keeps them.

—Psalm 119:129

The entrance of Your words gives light; It gives understanding to the simple.

—Psalm 119:130

I opened my mouth and panted, For I longed for Your commandments.

—Psalm 119:131

Look upon me and be merciful to me, As Your custom is toward those who love Your name.

—Psalm 119:132

Direct my steps by Your word, And let no iniquity have dominion over me.

—Psalm 119:133

Redeem me from the oppression of man, That I may keep Your precepts.

—Psalm 119:134

Make Your face shine upon Your servant, And teach me Your statutes.

—Psalm 119:135

Righteous are You, O Lord, And upright are Your judgments.

—Psalm 119:137

Your word is very pure; Therefore Your servant loves it.

—Psalm 119:140

Your righteousness is an everlasting righteousness, And Your law is truth.

—Psalm 119:142

I cry out with my whole heart; Hear me, O Lord! I will keep Your statutes.

—Psalm 119:145

I cry out to You; Save me, and I will keep Your testimonies.

—PSALM 119:146

I rise before the dawning of the morning, And cry for help; I hope in Your word.

—PSALM 119:147

Hear my voice according to Your lovingkindness; O LORD, revive me according to Your justice.

—PSALM 119:149

Consider my affliction and deliver me, For I do not forget Your law.

—PSALM 119:153

Plead my cause and redeem me; Revive me according to Your word.

—PSALM 119:154

Great are Your tender mercies, O LORD; Revive me according to Your judgments.

—PSALM 119:156

Consider how I love Your precepts; Revive me, O LORD, according to Your lovingkindness.

—PSALM 119:159

The entirety of Your word is truth, And every one of Your righteous judgments endures forever.

—PSALM 119:160

I rejoice at Your word As one who finds great treasure.

—PSALM 119:162

Seven times a day I praise You, Because of Your righteous judgments.

—Psalm 119:164

Great peace have those who love Your law, And nothing causes them to stumble.

—Psalm 119:165

Let my cry come before You, O Lord; Give me understanding according to Your word.

—Psalm 119:169

Let my supplication come before You; Deliver me according to Your word.

—Psalm 119:170

My lips shall utter praise, For You teach me Your statutes.

—Psalm 119:171

My tongue shall speak of Your word, For all Your commandments are righteousness.

—Psalm 119:172

Let Your hand become my help, For I have chosen Your precepts.

—Psalm 119:173

I long for Your salvation, O Lord, And Your law is my delight.

—Psalm 119:174

Let my soul live, and it shall praise You; And let Your judgments help me.

—Psalm 119:175

As you allow God to speak to you through His Scriptures with His amazing teachings you will come to understand that it is acceptable to inquire of the Father and ask Him to remember in order to receive your blessing. Renew your mind to that of Christ Jesus. Let go of the old, and be ready to receive the new. He has so much more in store for you!

8
RENEWING
YOUR MIND

T HERE ARE TIMES to declare instead of petition,
though petitioning is in the comfort zone of
most believers. Most of us have been taught that
petitioning is holy, right, and reverent. This means that
while learning to declare and change our way of praying
we are going to have to renew our mind along the way
and remove some of the old patterns and teachings that
have been instilled in us. Over the years we become set
in our ways and comfortable with what we have always
known about prayer and the way we've been taught. We
are unfamiliar with what it will look like if we change.

Change can be difficult and challenging for some to
embrace. Oftentimes people would rather keep their
emotional bondage when they come to me for a session.
They don't know who they will be or what their lives will
look like without the issues they have suffered with for
years. People have a fear of man and a need to please other
people. Lifelong rejection mind-sets can be difficult to let

go of. People are afraid of change, afraid of what it will look like and what people will think.

It can be the same with learning how to pray differently. To start praying out loud in front of people and change the way they pray can become an obstacle people have to work to overcome. The ability to pray in front of people is something I hope you will all want to obtain someday. However, for purposes of this book, at this moment I am just trying to get you to pray out loud in your own prayer time. Hopefully the rest will come as a natural byproduct of what you learn through declaring and as you gain boldness in Christ Jesus.

In order to renew our minds I believe Romans 8 has a lot to show us about living a life in the spirit, serving, and co-laboring with the Spirit of God. In Romans 8:4 it says, "Do not walk according to your old nature" (author's paraphrase). Our old nature is our flesh. It is our old life and sinful desires. Even though prayer is not a sinful desire, we need to learn not to walk in the old ways but in the new ways, being led by the Spirit. Our old ways want to please the flesh. Pleasing the flesh can entail rebellion, disobedience, and control. When a teacher is instructing us in a new way to do things our flesh can arise and say, "But I've always done things this way. I know best." "It works for me. Why should I try something different?" Or, "Don't tell me how to pray." As we grow older we become set in our ways, and we feel we do know best. Rebellion and control can come and activate against others and God. If the Holy Spirit is nudging you toward a different way to pray, and you keep ignoring it, you are acting in rebellion and disobedience. You are saying, "God, I know better than You, and my way is the right way."

As I said before, change can be difficult. Our mind needs to be renewed to walk in the spirit. When we read in Romans about walking in the spirit it is speaking of our mind, not our outward actions, even though it is a good idea to have those also be in the spirit. Walking in the spirit is living a life according to the desire of the Holy Spirit in a way pleasing to Him. It is taking every thought captive, submitting that thought, and making that thought obey Christ. (See 2 Corinthians 10:4-5.) When we search out the scripture in 2 Corinthians that discusses taking every thought captive it is specifically referring to rebellion and pride. In prayer that is where we can get caught up and not able to move on. Rebellion and pride say, "It's my way or the highway." Pride says, "I can't be taught something new because I already know it all. I should be teaching you." The last thing we want to become as Christians is unteachable.

We often fulfill what we set our affections toward. We need to make sure that we remain moveable and teachable even though we have our mind set in a certain direction. If we don't take our mind and thoughts captive we will identify ourselves with our old nature instead of the new creation we have become "in Christ" (2 Cor. 5:17). Notice the small filler word here: *in* Christ. We are in Christ. We are one in Him, and He is one in us. We are in union with Christ Jesus, the Messiah. When we renew our mind to the identification that we are in Christ, then we will set our mind on the things of the Spirit and not the comfort of our own flesh.

It is a conscious choice to focus on things of the Spirit. The enemy comes at us several times a day with thoughts he wants us to believe that are lies. It can become difficult not to concern ourselves with what other people think because the thoughts in our mind tell us otherwise. If we are not casting down such thoughts we are in disobedience to God's Word and are allowing a stronghold to be built up within ourselves.

Romans 8:6 reminds us, "For to be carnally minded is death, but to be spiritually minded is life and peace." When we are controlled by our old nature and mind-binding thoughts we are being unproductive. It is paralyzing because we focus our mind more on our old self and on old ways than the new ways that the Spirit is leading us in. However, when we yield to and allow the Holy Spirit to instruct us and lead us there is life and peace. Yielding requires a conscious effort on our part to not say that we know best and to recognize that He knows best.

When Jesus left He gave us the Comforter. I am so grateful that He left us the Spirit of God to co-labor with us. The Spirit of God intercedes and co-labors in prayer with us, but let's break down the following well-known verse and discover what it truly says.

> Likewise, the Spirit also helps in our weaknesses. For we do not know what we should pray for as we ought, but the Spirit Himself makes intercession for us with groanings which cannot be uttered. Now He who searches the hearts knows what the mind of the Spirit is, because He makes intercession for the saints according to the will of God.
>
> —ROMANS 8:26-27

The Holy Spirit takes part with us when we pray. He co-labors with us and makes our prayers effective. Think of it this way: Sometimes you start to pray and don't know exactly what to pray, but you pray anyway, struggling over the words. However, as you continue to pray, all of a sudden something happens, and the anointing kicks in or revelation starts to drop into your spirit about what you should be praying for and saying. All of a sudden you stop fumbling over your words and discover that you are flowing in a fervent prayer, calling things forth and knocking down spiritual strongholds. That is the Holy Spirit co-laboring with you in prayer.

The Holy Spirit knows the will of God and therefore can assist us in praying according to the Father's will. As we receive revelation from Him we will know what God's will for our life is and be able to pray accordingly, with power and authority. The Holy Spirit instills in us proper desires. He lines our prayers up with His and tells us what to pray for so that our heart and His are perfectly in sync.

> May He grant you according to your heart's desire, And fulfill all your purpose.
> —Psalm 20:4

Who better to know our purpose than the Spirit of God Himself? With the Holy Spirit co-laboring with us He will strengthen our inner man (Eph. 3:16).

Legalism is defined as "strict, literal, or excessive conformity to the law or to a religious or moral code." Legalism is one of the elements of religion that has to be rooted out of our lives in order to grasp the concept of praying differently through declarations. Legalism is rooted in laws and in the idea that we should do things in the way we have always done them. However, when we look at the Bible we can see clear outlines of the power of our words and speaking out into our situation. Our churches and church leaders haven't taught us about declaring, so legalism will give us the idea that we shouldn't do things that way. That is where you may have old mind-sets to overcome.

We need to eradicate the mentality that Christians can't have nice things and make a demand on the spiritual realm for things to come forth. God wants us to prosper and be in health. He wants us to have prosperity, not so much for personal gain but because the more we have, the more we can give away to others. People struggle to tithe ten percent of their income, but my husband and I want a lot of income so we can live on the tithe of 10 percent and give the other 90 percent away. Now, that's going to take a lot of money.

We have been taught as Christians to live menially, that we should lack and not have a lot. That couldn't be further from the truth. This is a distorted message in the body of Christ. Jesus talked about finances more than anything else in the Bible. Why should we be worried about money all of the time? When we lack we worry about money. Worry is a sin. Shouldn't we have more than enough so that the sin of worry doesn't consume our mind and make us unproductive and unfruitful?

Unworthiness is one of the factors preventing us from receiving and believing that we have the right to receive. Christians have a receiving problem. We go to a restaurant or a coffee shop, and we squabble over who is going to pay the bill. Your friend says, "I'll get it." You respond, "No, I'll get it," and you go back and forth until somebody caves. That is a receiving problem. If you can't receive a five-dollar latte how are you going to receive something much greater from God?

If you can't receive a meal being paid for, how are you going to claim, command, and decree and then expect to receive what you are declaring? You won't feel worthy to receive it or believe God can or should do it for you. Unworthiness is rooted in not knowing who you are in Christ. You are a son or daughter of God, and just because of that you deserve to receive. Christ is living in you, the hope of glory. The very Spirit of the living God is in you, and because He is in you and He is worthy, you know what? That makes you worthy. It's a plain and simple message yet a profound message that the body of Christ needs to grab hold of.

God loves you. He created you in His image. You are created in the likeness of God. That is a reason to celebrate the victory that you already have inside of you. His very likeness is in you! Again, people haven't been able to come to this deep realization because they haven't heard it preached from the pulpits. I'll say it to you: You are worthy! When is the last time you screamed out that you are worthy, that you are loved and wanted, and that you deserve everything coming to you simply because you are a son or daughter of God? You don't have to do anything; you just have to receive it. What is it going to take to renew your mind to receive that?

One time God had to renew my mind to receive as I went on a ministry trip and stayed with a lady I had just met. We were eating dinner when she excused herself from the table. Upon returning, she said, "Your bath is ready." I asked, "What?" She didn't even know how much I loved baths. When I went up to her bedroom suite in her house she had drawn me a bath with candles and fountains and music playing. She told me the proper order of going into the Jacuzzi, tanning bed, sauna, and shower and had everything perfectly set up for me. I got situated in the tub, and tears streamed down my face as I felt God's love pour out on me. He treated me so lavishly.

You see, I had a receiving problem and had to learn how to receive. I had many other blessings that weekend that were all perfectly set up by God to show me that I was a princess in His kingdom and that I deserved to receive. I remember it vividly and still preach about it today. The warmth of His radiance shining down on me and that same overwhelming love and reception from Him is available to you because He loves you. You are worthy to receive everything He has for you.

It can be difficult to grasp your identity in Christ and that you are entitled to what Christ has and did. It takes a different belief system than the one we were raised in, but as we study the Scriptures we find that God desires this for us.

There is a correlation between what happens in the natural and what happens in the spiritual, and vice versa. When we are declaring we are taking something that has happened in the spiritual and calling it forth to manifest in the natural.

When praying for healing we call and claim forth our healing based on many scriptures but especially the scripture, "By His stripes we are [I am] healed" (Isa. 53:5; see also 1 Pet. 2:24). We may not currently see the manifestation of our healing, but we are claiming and decreeing the finished work of the Cross in faith and considering it finished and complete. Our healing and deliverance have been purchased and accomplished in the heavenly spiritual realms. By declaring we are saying in faith that we believe and now expect to receive. There is a natural spiritual correlation.

God can give us a dream or vision to show us what has been released in the spiritual realm. That vision can give us discernment as to what to proclaim in the natural realm. When declaring, it is important to know His will and His Word and line your declarations up with the visions and knowledge that He has given you. We don't want to go around loosely declaring but rather lining our will up to His. When we do we will see the spiritual manifest to the natural.

As you declare you are prophesying into your future. You are speaking into existence what you believe will happen. Prophets prophesy into our lives, and we believe we will see the fruit of those prophesies. We are a prophetic generation and can be speaking into our own lives as much as we do others. I encourage the people I minister to, to write a prophetic declaration at the beginning of each year. Prophesy into your future what you want to see happen. Write a declaration to call out and claim forth:

I will be prosperous.

My children will come to know the Lord and serve Him.

My financial situation will change. I will become debt free, and the financial increase will come.

My job will be stable and provide the hours and finances I require.

My vehicle will be and continue to stay in good working order.

My body will strengthen with every step I take and every breath I breathe.

My spouse will have favor and abundance in all they do.

Our church will grow and be able to minister to more people.

No weapon formed against me and my family will prosper.

Revelation and visions will be in abundance, and I will grow spiritually.

Think about what you need to happen and what you desire to see. Speak to your circumstances and what needs to be released into your life, marriage, and ministry.

When we search the Scriptures we can discover that they prayed *saying.* This means that they prayed out loud. It is important if we are going to renew our minds to make sure that we are following the biblical examples found in the Scriptures of how they prayed. If you are someone struggling with legalism, then you definitely want to see where this theory is found in the Bible.

We see in the verses below that when Hezekiah prayed, he prayed to the Lord *saying.* These were outspoken words. He didn't pray in his mind—thinking, meditating, or pondering. It clearly states that he prayed to the Lord *saying.*

> Then he turned his face toward the wall, and prayed to the LORD, saying.
> —2 KINGS 20:2

> For a multitude of the people, many from Ephraim, Manasseh, Issachar, and Zebulun, had not cleansed themselves, yet they ate the

Passover contrary to what was written. But Hezekiah prayed for them, saying, "May the good LORD provide atonement for everyone."

—2 CHRONICLES 30:18

Then Hezekiah prayed to the LORD, saying.

—ISAIAH 37:15

David and Moses, two great men of God, prayed out loud. In both of these scriptures, we read that they prayed by speaking out with their words:

So Moses cried out to the LORD, saying, "Please heal her, O God, I pray!"

—NUMBERS 12:13

Then someone told David, saying, "Ahithophel is among the conspirators with Absalom." And David said, "O LORD, I pray, turn the counsel of Ahithophel into foolishness!"

—2 SAMUEL 15:31

Jesus also prayed *saying*. Actually, three times in the same passage of Scripture we find Him praying to the Father. I just can't imagine Jesus communicating any other way.

He went a little farther and fell on His face, and prayed, *saying*, "O My Father, if it is possible, let this cup pass from Me; nevertheless, not as I will, but as You will"....Again, a second time, He went away and prayed, *saying*, "O My Father, if this cup cannot pass away from Me unless I drink it, Your will be done"....So He left them,

went away again, and prayed the third time,
saying the same words.
—Matthew 26:39, 42, 44, emphasis added

What can be confusing and sometimes bring on feelings of condemnation is how much you are praying versus how much you are declaring. Those who have been bound in legalism may believe that there are rules or rituals pertaining to how to declare. They can begin to feel ashamed that they are not doing it well enough. These are some of the old mind-sets from the way people were raised. You tried to please your parents, spouse, or friends, and it was never good enough, so now you are wondering if you are embracing this new prayer life well enough. The answer is yes!

When self-condemnation attempts to come in and infiltrate your mind and prayer life, smash that thought down and replace that lie with the truth of God's Word: "There is therefore now no condemnation to those who are in Christ Jesus, who do not walk according to the flesh, but according to the Spirit" (Rom. 8:1). You are walking in the Spirit. Therefore, what you do and how you pray is good enough.

As we study this verse we learn that we are not condemned. In the Complete Jewish Bible it says that we "are in union with the Messiah Yeshua." When I think of union, I think of something that is intertwined. Christ's Spirit is in us, and we are in Him. Therefore, if there is no condemnation in Christ Jesus, then there is no condemnation in us. Once we give our life to Christ we don't walk in the flesh but in the Spirit. Since we don't walk in the flesh we shouldn't take on the attitudes of the flesh, such as self-condemnation. I know we do, but we shouldn't. As we renew our mind it should be that easy to tell ourselves, if we have to, that we no longer have to struggle with fleshy emotions because we are engrafted in Christ. (See Romans 11.) We come from His vine, and condemnation doesn't live in His plant!

Part of Romans 8 is about walking in the Spirit. As we walk in the Spirit we have to choose consciously to take each thought captive that does not line up with who we are and whose we are. When we received Christ we received deliverance, and as we grow in our Christian walk freedom continues to be released into us. This freedom we receive is in our mind, where the battlefield is. Therefore, as a thought comes in dismiss it and say, "That is not who I am."

Throughout our entire lives our parents and other influences have taught us who we are. The circumstances around us have molded our thinking. We have had people teach and train us in their ways, and they crafted us into their image instead of God's image. We have a lifetime of teaching and input to redo and reconstruct. And as I was praying I felt that God wants us to recreate, repurpose, and redesign some things in our lives. This is what He shared with me. Take some time and meditate on it. Think about how you can *re-* your life.

PROPHETIC WORD ABOUT REPURPOSING

I was spending time in prayer and the presence of God when I began to experience words such as *replant, rebuild,* and *refurbish* being released in my spirit. I felt that the Spirit of the Lord was telling me that He was going to be repurposing His people. It was going to be a time of *re-* words, including *recreating* and *rebuilding.* I couldn't help but think that the word *revival* also begins with the prefix *re-*.

Refurbishing an item involves stripping it down to its bare material and repainting it. It requires much work sometimes to take off all of the layers of old paint, to sand it down, smooth it out, and prepare it to be painted and beautified. It is a perfect analogy of what our Father does to His people in order to get them ready to be useful and productive for His kingdom. An old item such as a crate or a chair can still be used before it is sanded down and town apart. It may be chipped and peeling, and some pieces may be falling off. But, after it is chipped away at and the old paint scraped off it can be varnished or painted again, not only making it appear beautiful but this time radiating a beauty so that everyone now wants that product.

Our master Creator can do that with us too. He can scrape away the pieces that don't beautify us or represent His name well. He can chip away at us through conviction, instruction, and directions. His Spirit can reveal to us where we need to put away the old and take on the new.

I am hearing that out of *re-* newness things you thought were lost, washed away to the sea, or had no hope for anymore will be rebuilt and replanted in your life, and it begins with the refurbishing.

Imagine for a moment an item being refurbished. It has some bare wood showing and paint now peeling off. Now envision the product done, painted with a new coat, perhaps with some designs on the top layer. God was creative when He made this world with the trees, oceans, mountains, and all of the natural beauty that He gave us to enjoy. Our God has made the world so beautiful with all of the different kinds of trees and shades of green. He made the lakes and oceans, beautiful bodies of water, and created the sound of the waves crashing up against the shore for your enjoyment. He made the stars to glisten at night so that as you gaze out into an open sky you can see the beauty of the wondrous works of His hands. How much more would He choose to recreate you, His very own child, into someone magnificent for His glory and the representation of His name?

As we are recreated, replanted, and rebuilt, we will be beautiful. Just as someone may not have wanted the old box or chair, once it is refurbished, all of a sudden it becomes a cherished, valued, wanted item. You are all that to God—even without the refurbishing! You are cherished, valued, wanted, and loved greatly by Him. Don't you want to allow Him to come in and take those wounds—the hurt, pain, unfairness, and areas of your life where you are uncomfortable—and allow Him to refurbish them? He can do it. The question is, Will you allow Him? A piece of furniture doesn't have a choice whether or not to be refurbished, but God gives us free will. He gives us a choice whether or not we will allow ourselves to be recreated. What will your choice be?

Upon us is a time of restoration, of restoring things that were once lost, of repurposing those who feel they have no purpose, and recreating people to be all they need to be for the master Creator and His kingdom.

9
EVERYTHING
IN ORDER

G OD IS A God of order. As with everything in the kingdom, there is a God-ordained plan of events when we begin to confess, declare, and decree.

For me, the manifestation of my confession that I would have a Dodge Charger started as favor, and it turned into a desire of my heart. I started speaking by faith my desire to have it. It turned into a word of knowledge from God that I would have it. I took the word of knowledge and declared it out of my mouth. Believers came alongside me in the power of agreement. God sent people to provide the financial blessing. I prayed for discernment. I trusted God for the manifestation of His promise—and He was faithful! He is faithful.

God wants to give His children good gifts: "If you then, being evil, know how to give good gifts to your children, how much more will your Father who is in heaven give good things to those who ask Him!" (Matt. 7:11). God longs to grant us the desires of our heart when our desires line up with His will.

> May He grant you according to your heart's desire, And fulfill all your purpose.
>
> —Psalm 20:4

The Word states, "And we know that all things work together for good to those who love God, to those who are the called according to His purpose" (Rom. 8:28). When good things work together His name gets glorified! God longs to give us things that will glorify His name and bring the testimony of Jesus Christ forward.

In learning how to declare, as I was in a time of prayer the Holy Spirit showed me through revelation the proper order. As I preached a sermon one Sunday, the Spirit started speaking out through me this outline for declaring. He is the Great Instructor, and I believe that as we progress forward in learning declaration we can see things manifest in our lives.

THE ORDER OF DECLARING

Presence

In order to know what the will of God is for your life and the situation or item you need to be instructed to declare out, you need to get into the presence of God. You can get in the presence of God through reading the Word of God, prayer, worship, or soaking.

The Word of God

Reading the Bible assists us in knowing what the will of God is for our life. As we read stories of people in the Bible we can receive revelation from the Spirit that will help us relate to a character. When we relate to that person, we may get an unction that we want to be like them. As we continue to pray and fast God could show us that our calling is similar to a certain person in the Bible.

It is not just about our calling. Perhaps a person in the Bible had faith to bring someone to Jesus for their healing. That specific story might speak to you, and you might realize that you desire that same kind of faith. There are many stories of faith in the Bible. The woman with the blood issue had faith (Matt. 9:20). The centurion had faith (Matt. 8:8). The woman who petitioned for her daughter's deliverance also had faith (Matt. 15:28). Start declaring that you will have supernatural faith and receive healing!

Worship

God can and does speak to us through worship. As we lift up His name and exalt the One who sits on the throne we can receive words of knowledge, visions, and instruction. If you desire to get in the presence of God, worship Him. Don't wait until Sunday or your next church service. Turn on some music and worship Him in the privacy of your own home.

Prayer

In prayer, and specifically in listening prayer, God can reveal our destiny and tell us what direction to go in or what He desires to give us physically or as a spiritual impartation. When in prayer be careful that you don't do all the talking. Take time to wait upon God and listen to Him. This is best described as entering into a time of silence and solitude. Each morning I spend fifteen minutes in pure quiet, connecting with the Father spirit to Spirit. I sit there in quiet before my mind fills with the busyness of the day. I focus on my spirit man so I don't get distracted, and I make myself available simply to rest and focus my mind on Him and connecting with Him in the early hours of the morning. In those times I will receive instruction and revelation on how to direct my day, or I will receive a direction for my ministry.

Soaking

Soaking is listening to soft, worshipful music or instrumental music, disconnecting with the world, and connecting with God. Again, it is making yourself available for the Spirit of the Lord to speak to you while you are not busy and being distracted. During this time you can lie prostrate on the floor or you can sit back in your comfy chair. Don't get too comfortable and fall asleep. You can even soak in a bathtub and focus on the Father. Making yourself still and restful before the Lord will allow you to enter into His presence and hear from Him.

When you first start to soak it will take you ten minutes or more to disconnect your mind from thinking about everything you have to do or did today. But after you consistently do it you will notice it becomes easier to connect with the Father, and you will start to receive revelation. (Learn more about soaking and connecting with God through worship in my book *A Worship-Woven Life: Learning to Live a Life of Praise*.) However, you are receiving from God and entering into His presence. Eventually you will receive a word of knowledge. God desires to give us direction in our lives concerning what He intends for us. As you receive words of knowledge write them down. Wait until the Holy Spirit instructs before you act upon them.

Receive a Word of Knowledge

Words of knowledge can come in different ways. You can receive a word of knowledge through time spent with God, as I have discussed. You can also receive a prophetic word from a prophetic person. Both spending time in the presence of God and receiving a word directly from God or a prophetic person are valid. When receiving a word from a prophetic person make sure to test it against the Scriptures and weigh the character of the person delivering the word. Seek out the fruits of their ministry in order to make sure they give credible words.

Words of knowledge can also manifest through a desire of our heart or something that we know is God's will for our life. When we have a desire in our heart we should test it out to see if it scripturally lines up. The Bible is full of wise instruction, and when we take a desire and ask ourselves if it lines up with Scripture we will find the answer.

Prayer in Regard to Word of Knowledge

Now that you have verified that the word of knowledge lines up with Scripture, take it to prayer. Make sure it is the will of the Father for whatever you are declaring out. If you are declaring out healing, then search healing scriptures. We know it is His will to heal. If you are seeking out a possession, then study what the Bible says about prosperity. If you believe you are called to ministry, then search out the qualifications of a minister. His Word will give you the answer to everything you need.

We should use Jesus' example when He was in the garden as a guideline for the Father's will. Jesus, knowing He was going to be persecuted, said, "Not My will":

> He went a little farther and fell on His face, and prayed, saying, "O My Father, if it is possible, let this cup pass from Me; nevertheless, not as I will, but as You will."
>
> —MATTHEW 26:39

Use Jesus as a great example, and make sure that even though you have a desire ultimately you care about God's will more than you do your own.

Take the word of knowledge and ask yourself and discern if the name of Jesus will be glorified through it. The end result should be that the name of Jesus is held high and lifted up through the testimony and not that our pride is elevated with the seeking of attention and self-exaltation. When His name is glorified and He knows that the intention of your heart is to glorify His name and not exalt yourself through what you are declaring, He will move heaven and Earth on your behalf.

Pray and ask the Father to show you the next steps. What you hear could vary. He may tell you to rest and wait on His timing. That is difficult to do after you received revelation of something that is coming, but often we learn in the waiting period. Take whatever instructions He is giving and co-labor with them. That's right! We often don't think we have a role to play in it, but we do. Most of the time God isn't going to drop a million dollars in your lap, but He may call you to start a business and will give you the million dollars that way. People get an instruction and believe that God will supernaturally make it happen, but we have to co-labor through prayer, waiting, and being in the right place at the right time to receive the divine appointment or connection. Be sensitive and in tune to the voice of the Spirit so that you can act when He says to act.

Speak It Out

Speak out loud through prayer and declarations what God is desiring to manifest in your life. There is power in the words that we speak out into the spiritual atmosphere. Angels and demons are literally waiting to carry out assignments on our words. Let's activate the spiritual realm in positive ways with our words.

Use Scripture to speak out your desire to see the word of knowledge manifest. Find a Scripture to attach to what you are believing for, and speak it out along with claiming your healing, possession, or ministry position. Anything can be declared out. When we hear what we are claiming out loud, it builds up our faith: "So then faith comes by hearing, and hearing by the word of God" (Rom. 10:17). There is much truth in hearing out loud what we believe and desire to see increase or manifest.

You can speak out loud such declarations as:

I claim my financial situation is improving.

I speak to my body and tell it to be restored.

I say God will equip me for every good work for His ministry.

Declaring can apply to general things we need too. So often we don't know how to pray for our finances or about the infirmity in our body. We can get stuck in worrying or praying the same thing. We can get our mind focused in a negative direction, which is unproductive. By speaking out the opposite of what you are experiencing, you are declaring that change to come forth into the natural. You are focusing on a positive direction instead of a negative direction. Therefore, you can take what you know in the natural and turn it into a positive declaration with what you are hoping for or attach a Scripture to the circumstance and declare it out.

I spoke out loud every time I saw a Dodge Charger. I said, "I will have a Dodge Charger, in Jesus' name." Again, though, I want to emphasize that I spoke it out and declared it because it started as a desire of my heart and God gave me a word of knowledge on it. I don't believe that everyone who speaks out that they will have a certain kind of car will see the manifestation of their words.

Authority

We have been given authority, and now that we have a word of knowledge we need to take authority over that possession. Take authority over the spiritual realm. Command out loud that there will be no delays, distractions, or detours on your assignment in Jesus' name. Command all hindrances and lack to go in Jesus' name. Call forth every good and perfect gift from above to come forth and materialize in the name of Jesus.

There is possession in our confession. When we confess out loud with faith, belief, and trust in accordance with His will, it will happen. We will possess when we confess. So, what are you going to confess out today? Remember, "Death and life are in the power of the tongue, And those who love it will eat its fruit" (Prov. 18:21). As we confess, let's make sure we are calling forth those things that are not, in Jesus' name.

Faith

When you are calling forth something that doesn't currently exist you've got to have faith.

> So the Lord said, "If you have faith as a mustard seed, you can say to this mulberry tree, 'Be pulled up by the roots and be planted in the sea,' and it would obey you."
>
> —LUKE 17:6

Take the faith as a mustard seed, and nourish and grow it. Know that whatever you are expecting is for you. Realize that since you already discerned it, it is the will of God, and speak it out with faith. Do not doubt, as Jesus didn't doubt when He spoke to the fig tree (Matt. 21:21). He instructs us that if we don't doubt we can do the same to the fig tree, and we can command mountains to move.

A lot of the time a lack of faith is the obstruction to receiving blessings. Keep your faith by trusting, believing, and reading what the Bible says about trust and faith. Memorize the Scriptures and believe in your heart that you will receive. Know that God gives good gifts to His children, and you are one of His children, so He can give good gifts to you. It's often easier for us to believe for another person's blessing than for our own. God is no respecter of persons, and what He does for one He can do for another, "for there is no partiality with God" (Rom. 2:11).

Expect He Will Do It

Expectation is the breeding ground for miracles. Expect that God will do it. Don't allow vain imaginations or false scenarios to distort your thinking and get you off track. Don't give the enemy any room in your mind to create doubt and unbelief, but take every thought captive and submit it to the Word of God (2 Cor. 10:4-5). People have a mentality of not expecting so that when something happens it will be a real blessing, and if it doesn't happen they won't be disappointed. That is pessimistic thinking, and it's wrong! We should expect that the God who allowed Jesus to perform miracles while walking the Earth will continue to produce miracles through us today.

Believe

Keep pressing forward and believe for what you are expecting despite opposition. That's the definition of *perseverance*: "continued effort to do or achieve something despite difficulties, failure, or opposition." Not everyone is going to stand in agreement with you. Not everyone is going to believe for the impossible. Keep believing, because you have a promise from God. Don't quit! I have a saying—Defeat is not an option—and we know the saying that quitters never prosper. Have radical, crazy faith to believe that God can and will do the impossible. We live by faith not by sight. If no one will stand with you and believe, it's OK. You have the greatest team of three that are always standing by you: the Father; Jesus, the Son; and the Holy Spirit.

Receive

Learn how to receive now in the little things so that you can receive much more later on. Too few people, including Christians, know how to receive. God wants to bless us. When He chooses to use people and we argue back and forth about who is going to pay the bill, we rob people of receiving the blessing of being used by God. If we can't receive a five-dollar latte or a ten-dollar lunch from someone, how are we going to receive something of much more value?

I was one of those people who couldn't receive. God had to show me through a progression of events how to receive. Do you know what I discovered? I like to receive. I very much love to give presents. Both giving and receiving are my love language, but truly I love to receive. Allow people to bless you but always look to God as the Giver through the person.

Don't Give Up. Stand!

While waiting for your blessing to manifest, no matter what it is, don't give up. Are you waiting for an alcoholic child to stop drinking, a lost soul to come back to the Lord, or a promotion at work? Keep speaking it forth! Never stop believing! God can do the impossible. Lean on my son's favorite scripture: "I can do all things through Christ who strengthens me" (Phil. 4:13). You can do all things! Wait and stand in faith for what God is going to do in you and through you.

While I was waiting for my Dodge Charger to materialize there were some challenging moments. I wanted it so much; even now I don't know why I wanted it so badly. I can just tell you that I did. It hurt at times, desiring something so much and not knowing when it would manifest. I wanted it to manifest quickly because I knew in ministry that your following changes about every five years, and I had spoken about this desire and the power of declarations at my meetings as I traveled the United States. I wanted God's name to be glorified and people to realize the power of declaring. For this to happen the people I had spoken it out to had to see the manifestation, so I wanted it sooner rather than later.

I continued waiting on the Lord when the engine blew in one of our vehicles. We prayed about whether or not to purchase a vehicle, but I felt like God was saying to wait. I did not want to purchase a vehicle of any kind if this was God's chance for His name to be glorified through the Dodge Charger. We went months without a vehicle while I waited to know the voice of the Lord in this situation.

While we were awaiting direction from the Lord two of my adult children's vehicles also died; therefore, we had four adults sharing one vehicle. This was a hardship, but I was not going to buy a vehicle out of desperation.

During this time I got weary. I didn't see how it would happen. It was wearing on me to declare for something about which I didn't know the timing, so I tried to give up on the dream. I stopped declaring for six weeks out of frustration. I would drive by Dodge Chargers and choose not to speak it out because inside I was in turmoil. I believed. I knew I would have it. I just didn't know when or how. God spoke to me very sternly and said, "Kathy, if you give up on the dream of having a Dodge Charger you aren't giving up on the Dodge Charger; you are giving up on My ability to provide it for you." Ouch! I knew it was the voice of my Father! I repented, cried it out, and went back to believing in faith that it would manifest. And it did, only about five short months later, after I repented and started to declare again. The entire process—from my first declaration to manifestation—took two and a half years.

Around that time my husband and I felt a release to start looking at cars, and that is when I saw a Dodge Charger for about five thousand dollars. It was not perfect, not my dream, but I thought, "We have enough money to do this." However, it wasn't the one for us. We kept looking at cars, and I claimed out of my mouth just a few times, "God, I need about three thousand more dollars than what I have to get what I want." I finally knew God desired for all the gifts of money people had blessed me with, all of which I had put aside out of obedience to the Lord, to be for the Dodge Charger I had claimed out.

I knew what I wanted: a red, white, or black Dodge Charger with chrome wheels, no decals, and a spoiler. I began looking online for my car, but everything was out of the price range of what I had accumulated.

Then it happened. One day a person showed up at my door with a small gift bag filled with hundred-dollar bills totaling three thousand dollars—exactly what I had asked of the Lord! I had the money I needed! I started looking a little more but still found nothing. I saw a fair amount of Chargers, but nothing caught my eye.

One day as I was on the computer searching for cars I saw it! I feel in love instantly. I ran my laptop down the hallway to my husband, who was in bed studying the Bible. I said, "Honey, I found it! This is it! My spirit jumped! This is the one!" He was shocked because it was everything I didn't want. It was silver and had custom decals and custom black rims. He could not believe that was the car I wanted.

Needless to say, we purchased the car, and it was everything God wanted! He didn't want me to settle for a five-thousand-dollar Dodge Charger; He gave me a thirteen-thousand-dollar car! Remember, His name was to be glorified in this. My Dodge Charger was only five years old, had lower mileage, and leather heated seats (in front and back) with "Charger" embroidered in the front seats. It had custom tires, rims, and a custom grill. It has decals, my spoiler I wanted, and a sun roof! God wanted to go exceedingly abundantly beyond all I asked or was expecting!

When we were negotiating the price, we were approximately one hundred and twenty-five dollars short of it being free. The dealer wouldn't come down, and I was in so much turmoil it took me hours to make the decision. What I thought would be one of the greatest moments of my life was intense spiritual warfare. However, after much prayer, my husband and I both felt we should purchase it. I drove it home that day, and as I got home, my husband was led by the Lord to give me his fun money, which he had been saving for camera equipment. He had to the exact dollar amount, without even knowing it, that my car went over our budget, and he gave it to me.

I would like to encourage you to pray every step of the way while waiting for your blessing to manifest. So often we have a fleshly idea of what it should look like and how it should manifest. Some people might think a free car should come delivered to you with a big bow on it. Don't put God in a box. When I started the journey of looking for a car I didn't know if this was the time or season for the Charger, but as I patiently waited upon the Lord and kept discerning I followed His instructions, and He manifested the blessing.

Repent

When you get discouraged in the waiting process please remember my story and believe. Don't give up on God providing the dream! If He created the entire universe— and He did—He can fix your situation and bring to pass what you are waiting for. Repent of your unbelief and weariness and move on. Cry it out. Let out the emotions and fatigue you are feeling. Talk it out with Him. If you need to, go back to prayer again and verify that what you are waiting for is from Him. Sometimes we wrestle with God, wondering why He would make us wait and hope for something seemingly impossible. My suggestion is to take that moment of time if you need to, get it out of your system, and put God on the wrestling mat. Wrestle with Him, and then move out of that place from being a victim to being victorious.

Yet in all these things we are more than conquerors through Him who loved us.

—Romans 8:37

Scripture

Whatever you are believing for, search for scriptures that speak to that. If you are waiting for a person's salvation, then claim and call out scriptures on salvation, deliverance, redemption, and the lost coming home. If you are in need of a financial breakthrough, search out scriptures on prosperity. If you are seeking physical healing in your body, then find strength in scriptures that tell how Christ went around healing people. Look for other scriptures that talk about health, life, and healing. Attach several scriptures to your situation. The Bible is full of wonderful scriptural declarations. It is full of words to speak about your situation when you can't think of the words yourself.

Beloved, I pray that you may prosper in all things and be in health, just as your soul prospers.

—3 John 2

With long life I will satisfy him, And show him My salvation.

—Psalm 91:16

And my God shall supply all your need according to His riches in glory by Christ Jesus.

—Philippians 4:19

But He was wounded for our transgressions, He was bruised for our iniquities; The chastisement for our peace was upon Him, And by His stripes we are healed.

—Isaiah 53:5

Declare

Declare and start speaking out whatever you believe God is coming into agreement with and whatever He is revealing to you about what should manifest in your life or the life of another person. Call it forth at all opportunities. As I have said before, while I was waiting for my Dodge Charger every time I saw a Dodge Charger I would speak out loud, "I will have a Dodge Charger, in Jesus' name." It didn't matter if I was in the middle of a conversation, singing in my vehicle, or praying. I would stop and declare. Find a time, or do it as the Holy Spirit leads. Declarations are powerful, but they don't always have to come out powerfully. Statements of faith made simply have power because our God is a God of power. You can make statements of faith with pure intentions, with gentleness, and with a belief system that it will manifest. Call it out and declare it while driving, doing dishes, and walking. Speak into the spiritual atmosphere what you desire to see happen.

Power of Agreement

Solicit friends to come alongside of you and stand in agreement with you through declaring. The purpose of this book is to empower you to declare, not to ask people to pray for you. We all know how to pray for each other and how to ask people to pray. You want crazy-faith friends who will declare into the spiritual atmosphere with you.

While I was claiming out my Dodge Charger I was traveling the United States teaching on the power of declaring. People would hear my message, and some of those who had my cell phone number would stand in agreement with me. As they were going about their daily tasks, when they saw a Charger in a parking lot or on the road they would snap a picture and text it to me, telling me that they had just claimed it out loud for me. They would say into the spiritual atmosphere, "Kathy DeGraw will have a Dodge Charger." My team and I would be traveling, and as I would say, "I will have a Dodge Charger, in Jesus' name," another team member would say, "Give her one, God." Another team member would seal it in with, "Amen." There was power in agreement.

> For where two or three are gathered together in My name, I am there in the midst of them.
> —MATTHEW 18:20

Tithes and Offerings

The Bible instructs us to give our tithes and offerings. I believe as we financially give into the kingdom of God we will be blessed. The mentality of the church needs to change. People want to receive something without giving something. They say, "I can't afford to give." I say, "You can't afford not to give." I believe God will bless us when we give.

> "Will a man rob God? Yet you have robbed Me!
> But you say, 'In what way have we robbed You?'
> In tithes and offerings. You are cursed with a curse, For you have robbed Me, Even this whole nation. Bring all the tithes into the storehouse, That there may be food in My house, And try Me now in this," Says the LORD of hosts, "If I will not open for you the windows of heaven And pour out for you such blessing That there will not be room enough to receive it. And I will rebuke the devourer for your sakes, So that he will not destroy the fruit of your ground, Nor shall the vine fail to bear fruit for you in the

field," Says the LORD of hosts; "And all nations will call you blessed, For you will be a delightful land," Says the LORD of hosts.

—MALACHI 3:8-12

Right Standing with God

Being in right standing with God and making sure our motives are pure is important while waiting for our blessing. His Word says, "Blessed are those who hunger and thirst for righteousness, For they shall be filled" (Matt. 5:6). Invite the Holy Spirit in to work on the inadequacies in your life. I ask Him to "create in me a clean heart, O God, And renew a steadfast spirit within me" (Ps. 51:10). I ask him to "search me, O God, and know my heart" (Ps. 139:23). We need to make sure there is no manipulation, ulterior motives, or wrong intentions to what we are seeking.

Faithful and Obedient

Be faithful and obedient to God. Learn to live a life of faithfulness and fulfill His Word. Organize and restructure your life to live biblically, and discover ways to be faithful. Be obedient to His Word and His instructions. I have a saying called "first-time obedience." If God asks something of you, be obedient the first time and don't make Him ask again. Get into agreement with the will of God for your life and do everything in your power to be faithful and obedient.

Discipline

Be disciplined to study the Word of God daily. Have personal devotions and time in your secret place consisting of prayer and worship. When God gives you instructions, be disciplined to carry out those instructions. Write the instructions down and make sure you are obediently following those instructions.

Discipline is setting aside our self-will and acting on what God has for us. He is going to want to see you fulfilling His instructions before He gives you more. Why should He provide more revelation if you weren't disciplined to carry out the first set of revelation?

Discipline doesn't necessarily have to do with what you are specifically declaring for but refers more to all of the areas of your life.

Be Love

God's greatest commandment is to "love one another; as I have loved you, that you also love one another" (John 13:34). Simply put, be love. We are supposed to love one another as ourselves. Since we can't always do that because not everyone can love themselves, I encourage you to love as Jesus loved. See everyone as a son or daughter of God, because they are. Love them and treat them as if they are the most important person in the world. They are very important to our heavenly Father, and they should be very important to us. God will bless us as we extend the love of the Father simply because we desire to show people the love of God, which we have been shown ourselves. We don't love others to receive the blessing, but when we fulfill His command He will shower His blessings on us.

Pride

In order to receive God's blessings, pride must be rooted out. Put your pride on the altar and allow the Father to slaughter it. Again, ask Him to search you and create a clean heart within you. How are you going to receive the fullness of your blessing, elevation, or financial prosperity if you are going to go out shouting about it pridefully? Pride comes before the fall.

If we are to be love and show love toward God and people we need to do it in humility. It does us no good to receive a blessing if we are going to shove it in another's person's face in self-exaltation. The only thing we need to be exalting is the name of Jesus Christ. It is difficult to walk in humility, but if you allow God to have those areas of your life the testimony of your blessing will go far and wide for His glory.

No Idols

In general, when we are seeking something we look to man and try to figure out where it will come from. We point our finger at man and say that he has the money or the position to provide that blessing. When you do this, you look to man and not to God. We take our focus off of God and place it onto man.

Don't spend your time and energy looking to figure out where your blessing will come from. We will never know who or what God will use, but looking to man will focus our attention in the wrong direction.

> Suppose a man comes into your synagogue wearing gold rings and fancy clothes, and also a poor man comes in dressed in rags. If you show more respect to the man wearing the fancy clothes and say to him, "Have this good seat here," while to the poor man you say, "You, stand over there," or, "Sit down on the floor by my feet," then aren't you creating distinctions

among yourselves, and haven't you made
yourselves into judges with evil motives?
—JAMES 2:2-4, CJB

When I was waiting for my Dodge Charger the first
person that sowed a seed into it totally did it on their own.
They heard me preach one day. A week after that they
sent me a one-hundred-dollar seed. They planted into my
testimony when they were hurting for money themselves.
One of my last, larger donations actually came from a
person who was also in need of a vehicle. The person who
was in need of a vehicle themselves had actually told God
the month before that they wanted to bless someone with
a certain amount of money, which was coincidentally the
amount I needed.

Never assume where the money will come from because
God is the giver of gifts. God has it all planned out for us,
but we try to manipulate and idolize people. He doesn't
need your assistance to manifest your blessing.

Pray for Discernment

Remain in prayer while you are waiting for your blessing.
I believe there are times when we need to be in a certain
place at a certain time to make a divine connection or
receive our blessing. Therefore, I encourage you always to
be sensitive to the Holy Spirit's leading. Do you need to
go out to the coffee shop today or to a church meeting or
offer to volunteer at an event? Being sensitive and allowing
the Holy Spirit to direct our days will allow opportunities
to arise. Even though we don't want to idolize man and
look for man to bless us, most of the time God isn't
supernaturally going to drop what we are looking for into
our living room. Making ourselves available for divine

appointments and listening to when and where we should be will allow for those blessings to occur naturally.

Trust

Search out the Scriptures on trust and faith. When you look in the Bible at instances of the word *trust* you can put the word *faith* in its place, and vice versa. When you read the Complete Jewish Bible you see that the original text doesn't even use the word *faith* but *trust*. Trust God to bring it to pass. Trust God when all else says to fear and not to trust. Simply trust.

> Trust in the LORD with all your heart, and lean not on your own understanding.
> —PROVERBS 3:5

> The LORD is my rock and my fortress and my deliverer; My God, my strength, in whom I will trust; My shield and the horn of my salvation, my stronghold.
> —PSALM 18:2

> But as for me, I trust in You, O Lord; I say, "You are my God."
> —PSALM 31:14

> Commit your way to the LORD, Trust also in Him, And He shall bring it to pass.
> —PSALM 37:5

> Every word of God is pure; He is a shield to those who put their trust in Him.
> —PROVERBS 30:5

Receive the Promise

Receive the promise as it comes to pass. Give God the glory for whatever just happened in your life. Rejoice in the salvation of a lost loved one. Give Him the firstfruits of your promotion, job, or the sale of your home or vehicle. Point it all back to Him and share your testimony of faith and perseverance. Make sure that His goodness is known everywhere you go.

After I received my Charger my eighteen- and twenty-two-year-old children needed to drive it for one reason or another. Since it is a sporty looking car with decals, people ask about it. I would tell them it's OK if you drive it, but the one condition is that you tell whoever asks about the car the story of how your mom claimed this car for almost three years and how God provided this car for her absolutely free. That's my one condition for them to drive the car, so God gets all the glory every opportunity He can.

Encourage others to believe and hope for what they need to have changed in their life. Show them love and encourage them. Be their cheerleader and stand in agreement with them. I helped you along by writing this book. Now go and pay it forward. Assist another person on their way to freedom, victory, and prosperity. Share your testimony and be love in the process with humility, giving thanks to God for all things. And never forget what He did for you.

10
DEFINING
YOUR WORDS

WE USE WORDS to declare into the spiritual atmosphere. We have heard these words in the Christian community, words such as *declare, decree, command,* and *call forth.* When we look at these words they all appear to share a similar meaning. But what do they mean? In order to have a better understanding of what we are saying aloud so we know what words to use and when, let's define the words properly.

When writing and speaking aloud to make a declaration, we want to be wise. Wisdom comes from research. Solomon sought wisdom and received so much more. In his case, one of the things he received was wealth. I look at it as if we will gain spiritual wealth when seeking wisdom. When we are declaring, we want to be educated. As we learn how to define and properly use these words, people will have a better comprehension of what we are speaking in front of them in a prayer group or worship meeting. We can only put out with authority and power what we have put in; therefore, we need to be educated in what words to use and when to use them.

Here are the basic definitions with regard to declaring:

- *To proclaim* is to announce.

- *To call forth* is "to request to…come."[1]

- *To decree* is to command.

- *To command* is to order.

- *To establish* is to call to permanence.

TERMS TO USE WHEN SPEAKING OUT WITH AUTHORITY

Call forth: Calling things forth into the spiritual realm is powerful! *To call forth* means "to request to meet or come" and "to summon."[2] A court system can summon you and hand you a subpoena, and you must respond. You must come forth and answer the request. When you receive jury notification papers in the mail you must fill them out. When they call you must come. You have no choice but to respond. You have that same power. When you call forth into the spiritual realm with power and authority it must respond.

Command: *To command* means "to order," as well as "to direct, to send."[3] When we are commanding and ordering we are usually sending a person in a direction. This is done with firmness but authority. When you command, think about what direction you want to send angelic assistance in for help or in what direction you want to send demonic beings fleeing from your situation.

Declare: We declare to acknowledge possession or to manifest something we are calling forth. When we are declaring we are commanding an item to manifest in the spiritual realm. By speaking it out we are acknowledging possession. Even though we don't at the time see the results in the natural, we are acknowledging that we have possession of it in the spiritual realm, and we are requiring it to manifest in the natural.

Decree: To decree is to command; it is unchangeable. When speaking out decrees we must believe that they will be established. When we put our faith into alignment with the spiritual realm, the spiritual realm activates.

Dominion: *Dominion* is a word for "authority." Authority is the power to direct. It means that we have the right to possess. When Jesus ascended to heaven He transferred His authority to us. We have been given the right of possession. Instead of allowing unfavorable circumstances to control and direct us we have the authority to turn our situation around and have it submit to us, changing unfavorable conditions into favorable situations.

Establish: Establishing is a form of permanence. It is "to confirm...to settle or fix" permanently. What are you calling forth aloud from your mouth to establish permanently in the spirit realm? In Proverbs 18:21 it says, "Death and life are in the power of the tongue, And those who love it will eat its fruit." We can establish a lot by speaking out words, but what you have to realize about this verse is that whatever we speak out is what will bear fruit. If we speak positively we will bear the fruit of positive results. However, there is so much power in our tongue and the words that we speak that what we speak negatively can also produce negative results in our life. What are you going to establish with your words?

Instruction: Instruction is a "direction, order, command, [and] mandate."[4] Instruction is "calling for" direction or "compliance." Instead of us complying with instructions that are against us, let's give orders of instruction to the demonic realm to have their assignments backfire on them or call forth angels to labor on our behalf.

Obey: The command to obey is to command someone to yield. When you obey you submit to direction and comply with commands, orders, and instructions. As you obey you submit to direction. We have obeying powers against the enemy! We know how the word *obey* is defined, because as we are ordered into submission, most of us obey. It is wisdom to take this destroying power and make the spiritual realm obey us. There are attacks several times a day against us. We need to rise up in holy, righteous anger and combat those attacks with destroying powers by making the demonic realm submit to us.

Order: To order is "to manage...direct; to command."[5] It is to order troops. There are demonic troops in the satanic kingdom. The kingdom of darkness is organized, disciplined, and committed. The satanic kingdom is similar to a military group. A military group is dedicated to fulfilling their assignment. We need to have that same perseverance in us and order the spiritual realm around us until they are organized, disciplined, and committed to the instructions we deliver to them. We also need to keep declaring and ordering until we see the fulfillment of our promises, which means that we have to persevere and stay organized, disciplined, and committed ourselves.

Power: Power moves things or produces change. It is the "ability to act or produce an effect." Power is influence and strength. The scriptural definition of *power* is "right" and "privilege."[6] We have power over the enemy and our circumstances. God's Word says, "And when He had called His twelve disciples to Him, He gave them power over unclean spirits, to cast them out, and to heal all kinds of sickness and all kinds of disease" (Matt. 10:1).

Proclaim: When we proclaim, we are announcing. It is an official notice. Since we are given authority, we should take that authority and issue an official proclamation into the spirit realm of what we are decreeing. When the United States government announces the president walking into the room, people applaud; or when a king or queen enters a room, people bow. In either of these cases, the proclamation gets people's attention, and they respond. That is what should happen when you open your mouth and take authority; the spirit realm should respond. In all cases, someone has to open their mouth and proclaim who is walking into the room. In the case of declaring, it is you who has to proclaim something and announce it aloud.

Speak: To speak means "to pronounce...to declare, to proclaim...to exhibit, or make known."[7] In the spiritual realm both angels and demons are waiting to activate on our words. We must speak out how we want them to activate. *Speak* is an action word; we have something to do about our situation. We need to open our mouth, move our tongue, activate our vocal cords, and speak to our situation.

Speak out: We speak out many words a day, some productive and many unproductive. We would be wise to use our energy to speak productivity into the spiritual realm. To speak out is just that—speaking! We cannot be productive by just thinking about our situation. We need to speak to our situation to bring about a result or change.

Stand: Standing is maintaining "a specified position." When we stand, we are having the faith not to be overthrown. Standing is being determined to persevere and remain upright despite the warfare around us. We are believing to be continually fixed, to remain steady and unchanged. Standing is an important definition as we learn to wait for the manifestation of what we desire to see materialize.

Strength: Strength is "the application of force without breaking or yielding."[8] It is the "power of resisting attack." While declaring, you need strength. When God gives you a word of knowledge, a prophetic word, or something to stand and persevere on, you need to go forward in spite of opposition, which is standing with strength without breaking or yielding to the cause and mission you are declaring.

When specifically decreeing against the demonic realm it is important to utilize a variety of words in order not to be repetitive. To know what each word means will effectively assist you in inserting it into a declaration to be used against the demonic realm as a strong, punishing blow.[9]

Abort: To abort means "to stop something before it is completed because of problems or danger." The enemy wants to abort your assignment. He sends forth assignments against you to abort your commission. To stop demonic attacks of this nature, decree spirits of abortion against your destiny to be aborted in the name of Jesus.

Abolish: To abolish means "to completely do away with (something)." When you know the enemy is setting up specific attacks against you declare against it. You may say, "I command all assignments of the enemy to be abolished, in Jesus' name."

Annihilate: To annihilate is "to destroy" or "defeat" something "completely." When the enemy is building a plan against us we need to keep declaring until we have destroyed his plans completely. We move forward when we feel peace in the atmosphere and believe the attack is done.

Bind: Binding prevents "escape or movement." Jesus said to bind the strongman. (See Mark 3:27.) When the enemy is at work in a member of your family say aloud, "I bind and restrict (whatever the spirit's name is, such as anger) in Jesus' name. You will not activate in my family member or while they are near me. I take authority over you and bind you from activation in Jesus' name."

Break down: To break down is "to cause to fall or collapse by breaking or shattering; to make ineffective." The devil would like nothing better than to make us break down. We need to decree against him until he is ineffective in our mind, where the battle field is.

Call off: To call off means "to draw away." Call off all assignments of the enemy by simple statements and order him to draw away from you.

Cast out: To cast out is "to drive out" and "expel." Jesus cast the demons out. He didn't cast them off or allow them to hinder the person. He said, "Get out!" (See Luke 4:35.) Tell whatever is hindering you to get out in Jesus' name.

Cease: To cease means "to stop happening" and "to end." There are many things we can command to cease, like the enemy stealing, killing, and destroying our finances.

Confine: To confine means "to restrain."[10] Decide what needs to be confined and restrained. You can also use it along with the word *bind.*

Confuse: To confuse is to cause uncertainty or inability to understand something. I send confusion into the enemy's camp.

Constrict: To constrict means "to compress or to squeeze." The enemy is similar to a snake, and a snake constricts. He would enjoy constricting us, but instead we must constrict him with our words and put pressure on him to cease his assignments.

Deploy: To deploy means "to organize and send out (people or things) to be used for a particular purpose." Command angels to be deployed on assignment for a particular purpose.

Desecrate: To desecrate signifies damage. The thief wants to steal, kill, and destroy, which is damaging to the circumstances around you. When you send verbal decrees into the atmosphere you desecrate, damage, and infiltrate his camp so that he cannot activate against you.

Desist: Desist is a command "to stop doing something." *Desist* is a simple yet powerful word that can be used in a statement. Command the enemy to desist his activations against you in Jesus' name.

Demolish: Demolishing is "forcefully tear[ing] down" or taking "apart." In the natural people have forcefully torn us down with their words. The enemy often uses people, doing his bidding through them. He is forceful and continues with his plans and efforts. Be forceful against him and demolish him with your words.

Depart: To depart is "to go away," "to leave…a position." Give the enemy no credit, no room to exist. Tell the enemy aloud to depart from your region, ministry, or workplace. Tell him to go in Jesus' name!

Destroy: To destroy means "to cause (something) to end or no longer exist; to cause the destruction of (something); to damage (something) so badly that it cannot be repaired...to defeat (someone or something) easily or completely." Use the power of your words to destroy the enemy's attack against you. In the Bible it talks about how the kingdom of heaven suffers violence (Matt. 11:12). We need to get violent against the enemy and be diligent to destroy his powers over us.

Diffuse: To diffuse means "to pour out or cause to spread freely; extend, scatter...to break up and distribute." The devil and his demons are organized, committed, and disciplined. If you think about it, they are persistent and keep moving forward to destroy God's plans and prosperity against you. The words you speak need to diffuse his troops so that they are not committed and are disorganized.

Dispersed: To disperse means "to cause to break up...; to cause to evaporate or vanish." When you feel severe spiritual warfare attacks against you command them to disperse by the blood of the Lamb and in the name of Jesus.

Dissipate: To dissipate is "to cause (something) to spread out and disappear." Dissipate every evil troop that has been dispatched against you by speaking into the demonic realm. Call them forth to dissipate and cover that assignment with the blood of Jesus.

Dissolve: To dissolve means "to cause (something) to end or disappear." Dissolve all chaos and destruction against you. Command it to be dissolved. Sometimes we need to speak it out three times in a row to show our seriousness to dissolve and end those attacks.

Distribute: Distribute the blood of Jesus to enemy assignments. The blood of Jesus is a powerful tool to use while declaring. The devil knows that Jesus' blood was shed for us. As the song says, "There is power in the blood." Plead, distribute, and disperse the blood of the Lamb over your situation.

Disturbance: A disturbance indicates "a change in the position, arrangement, or order of something." Familiar spirits repeat the same happenings in a person's life or family line. Command disturbance to be sent into the enemy's camp to change his assignment against you.

Eradicate: To eradicate means "to remove (something) completely" or "to eliminate or destroy (something harmful)." People who are controlling, loud, and boisterous can sometimes be best related to by speaking loudly back to them. The enemy is the same way. Speak his language. Speak aloud firmly and eradicate his plans.

Incinerate: To incinerate is "to burn (something) completely." Incinerate the blueprints of hell against you.

Interrupt: To interrupt means "to cause (something) to stop happening for a time." We want to interrupt the plans of the enemy.

Nullify: To nullify is "to cause (something) to lose its value or to have no effect." Interrupt the enemy's plans and then nullify them by decreeing over them even more, causing them destruction.

Paralyze: To paralyze means "to make (someone or something) unable to function, act, or move." Paralyze the enemy's power above you, around you, and beneath you. Say, "I paralyze all demonic activity and assignments around me in Jesus' name."

Rebuke: To rebuke is to "keep down." Take authority over the enemy by rebuking him, but then give him a follow-up command. To rebuke is simply to take authority over; when taking authority, you have to give an additional instruction.

Refuse: To refuse means "to...not accept" or "not [be] willing...; to not allow...something." Refuse to accept natural diagnoses over your life and situations. In declaring, rebuke words spoken over you.

Remove: To remove is "to cause (something) to no longer exist; to force (someone) to leave a job." Remove the enemy from performing his actions against you. Decree so much that he wants to leave his job.

Renounce: To renounce means "to say in a formal or definite way that you refuse to follow [and] obey." Renounce any participation in following in the ways of the soul. Renounce any active participation in mind-binding thoughts that caused you to follow instead of taking authority.

Restrict: Restricting limits "the amount or range of (something)"; it "prevent[s] (someone) from doing something." The word *restrict* is best used with the word *bind*. Bind and restrict the enemy from activating within you.

Ruin: Ruin is "a state of complete destruction." Jesus completely ruined and destroyed the devil at the cross. You can destroy and ruin him with powerful declarations led by the Holy Spirit.

Scatter: To scatter is "to cause to vanish." Scatter the enemy's assignments and plans.

Thwart: To thwart means "to prevent (someone) from doing something or to stop (something) from happening." We've all heard the phrase "thwart the plans of the enemy." Now go forth and do so. Annihilate his camp.

Uproot: To uproot means "to remove (something) completely; to make (someone)... move to a different place." Uproot the enemy from our region, family, and territory. Command the blood of Christ and tell the enemy not to cross your borders.

Vanquish: To vanquish is to defeat someone completely in a war or battle. Jesus vanquished Satan, but we need to know our authority and identity to defeat him completely as he relentlessly tries to attack us.

Words are powerful as you declare and decree. The enemy means business! He is out to harm you and your family and cause the same patterns to repeat themselves. By learning how to decree and declare and by knowing an assortment of tactical words you can and will combat the attacks of the enemy.

11
WRITING A
DECLARATION

WRITTEN DECLARATIONS CAN flow from three different sources. You can assemble a declaration by natural insight, prophetic revelation, or scriptural adaption. As you are considering writing a declaration and you start thinking about where to begin I suggest first of all getting yourself connected with God and being in His presence. When we seek God through prayer or worship we welcome His glory, and where His glory resides, revelation becomes easy.

If you have never written a declaration prophetically (by the Spirit giving you revelation of what to write) or assembled one based on a particular need, then it is imperative that you spend time alone with God. Go into your prayer closet and pray. Seek Him on what to write and how to start. If you are not receiving, then pray in the spirit. When you pray in tongues your mind often shuts down, and then you can start receiving revelation.

Worship is one of the places where I get revelation from the Spirit of the Lord. Worship can be in many different forms. Worship can be putting on praise music and singing out to the Lord songs of praise and adoration with your hands lifted high. It can be worshipful music that really brings you into His presence and gets you on your knees before the throne of God. Prophetic music will usher you directly into the presence of God and get you on your face, prostrate before the Lord, ready to receive and hear from Him. No matter what type of worship you enjoy, go before the Father and worship Him in freedom, spirit, and truth. Connect with Him spirit to Spirit. You do know how you connect with Him best. Get in that place where you connect with Him in order to receive the revelation you need to write the declaration. (To learn more about receiving in worship, see my book *A Worship-Woven Life*.)

Have faith that the Spirit of the living God will give you the download you need. When I started receiving revelation I never tried to write a declaration. I had been declaring simple statement decrees out of my mouth for years. One day the Father shifted me and told me to pick up my pen, open my journal, and write by faith. He instructed me that each time I opened my journal in faith He would give me the revelation of what to write prophetically for a person, a specific topic, or a prophetic insight. I now have journals full of declarations for all sorts of circumstances, and so can you!

As you write declarations they can take on a different sound or pattern than mine. Don't expect all declarations to appear the same. God speaks to us all differently, and we all have different personalities in which to express ourselves and what we desire to convey. You may discover that some of what you receive to write is similar to the way you speak. You could receive repetitious things in different declarations with a similar theme. Whatever and however you write is OK. Everything is acceptable, whether you choose to write it out of natural insights or prophetic revelation. There is no right or wrong way to assemble a declaration. I am providing insights to begin for those who need it, but I believe in faith that you will someday sit down—maybe even today—and it will flow right out of you!

How might your declaration appear after you write it? Your declaration could appear as poetry, prose (in paragraph form), or as a list of statements.

Poetry

Your declarations assembled with natural writing skills or revelation from the Spirit could appear in poetry form. They may or may not rhyme and can appear in different formats of poetry. Don't try to rhyme your declaration while writing, but if a sentence or two comes out that way, leave it. You want to make your declaration as close as possible to what you were thinking or what the Spirit dropped into your spirit.

Prose

Prose is more natural and is defined by the Merriam-Webster Dictionary Online as "the language ordinary people use in speaking or writing." It is "a literary medium distinguished from poetry especially by its greater irregularity and variety of rhythm and its closer correspondence to the patterns of everyday speech." When we are writing a prophetic declaration, prose should flow naturally out of us through the Spirit of the Lord, though it is not something we aim to achieve or purposely attempt to write. On the occasions that it happens in our quiet time we will discover His words will flow out and end up being in the format of prose. It is not always achieved, but it something the Spirit of the Lord can release to use through our times of solitude, prayer, or worship.

Simple Statements or Sentences

Statements can be something you are naturally writing or prophetically writing from the revelation you are receiving. Write them as sentences in list form, all in one document. Do not attempt to put these in paragraph form; they are not meant to be. Don't try to make them coincide or fit together. They are intended to be spoken out as statements. They have individual character and, in the end, will accomplish what they need to in the spiritual realm.

Prophetic coincidence

Prophetic coincidences are declarations that can appear in the prophetic form. When you read them aloud to yourself or a group they can sound similar to a prophetic word. You have to discern during this time if it is actually a prophetic word or a prophetic declaration. A prophetic word is going to be released to the general public in the immediate moment, while a prophetic declaration will be kept in front of you to continually speak out in private.

RECEIVING AND RELEASING

During your time of seeking discernment on what to put on paper you may discover that it stirs your prophetic gifting. In Timothy it says to stir the gift within you (2 Tim. 1:6). You can stir those giftings by having the faith to believe and receive revelation. By being in prayer, worship, and praying in the spirit or tongues you stir up your gifting. Spending time in the presence of the Lord and waiting on Him to hear from Him will also stir up your gifting.

Therefore, if you are doing what the Bible instructs and believing by faith, why wouldn't this be an opportunity for your prophetic gift to flow, increase, and be released?

Keep your writings all in one place. It is helpful to purchase an oversized journal or a standard notebook. Smaller journals and pieces of paper will not keep your declarations all together and neatly organized. When writing declarations you will find that they will usually fill up one page of a larger piece of paper. Therefore, small journals and notepads are ineffective. You can even label your declarations with tabs that you can purchase. Stick the title out of the page for easy reference when preaching, praying, or seeking a declaration for a specific circumstance.

Take your declaration journal with you when you go places. You could receive revelation at church or in your secret place or during your Bible reading and study time. Keeping it with you always says, "God, I'm expecting." My team even knows to bring my journal to me if I have to reposition myself in a meeting. If I go under the power of the Spirit they will put it on the floor next to me in preparation for me receiving revelation.

When desiring to write a declaration, decide on the purpose of your declaration and the category it would fit best. Would it be easiest to write a natural insight, spiritual revelation, or scriptural adaption? Take a moment and ask yourself these questions: Could I write this based on what I know? Do I need to research the Scriptures? Do I need supernatural revelation on this topic and situation? When writing a declaration evaluate your motive and make sure it is pure and with the right intentions. Are you writing to control or change a person? Do you have soulish ambitions, or is personal gain or advancement involved? Do you desire to glorify the name of Jesus Christ?

All declarations should be examined to determine if the end result will glorify the name of Jesus Christ. If the end results point to Jesus and His kingdom, then declare away! If they don't you need to repent, self-evaluate, and seek the Holy Spirit for spiritual guidance and the godly direction to proceed in your circumstance. When you decree you are establishing a form of permanence in your life and in the lives of others. Therefore, you want to make sure when declaring that it is pure and by God's will and His Word. What do you want to be permanently established in your life? Decree it out!

Natural Insights

Writing a declaration with natural insights uses your knowledge, Bible verses you know, and things you have learned. Write these in sentence form to make your declaration. Take a natural circumstance and compound it with one of the words defined in Chapter 10. Adding one of the powerful words from the list I gave you will create power and authority in your declaration when used by faith.

When writing a natural declaration you generally will be starting with a topic. What kinds of topics will you be seeking? Seek a topic that coincides with a situation you are experiencing. Here is a list of topics you may want to write a declaration about:

- Disunity or dissension in marriage
- Concern about a job loss or layoff
- A medical diagnosis
- Addiction in a family member or yourself
- Calling forth good godly spouses for your children

- Spiritual warfare attacks

- Financial matters

- The release of ministry growth and destiny

- God's will to be done in the life of your children

- Infertility

- House or vehicle sale or purchase

You can write a declaration for anything that you need to call forth and bring into existence. This would be something that you would declare specifically. When my husband and I were declaring for our home we listed individually all of our needs for the house we were seeking. We declared forth a three-bedroom with an option of having available space or a room that we could renovate and turn into a fourth bedroom. We called forth a flat backyard with an open space that would allow us room to put up our above-ground pool. We called forth two sitting rooms on the main floor, one to be a living room and one to be a family room. We even called forth a fireplace for our family room. You know what we received? A three-bedroom house that is now a four-bedroom house with a pool in the backyard, a living room I can use as my secret place, and a family room with a wood–burning fireplace, just as we wanted! We received exactly what we declared.

That also happened when we were calling forth a vehicle. We declared specifically for what we were seeking. Do you want any used vehicle, or do you want a well-running used vehicle with no rust, good tires, and a CD player?

It is similar to praying in musicians for your worship team. Do you want any guitar player, or do you desire an anointed, gifted, and talented musician? Do you want your guitar player to come and just play music, or do you want a guitar player who is on fire for the Lord, someone who doesn't perform but worships, sharing and igniting their faith with everyone they come in contact with? Declaring specifically in faith will produce specific results and the results you desire.

I was ministering to ladies on social media who were desiring conception, so I decided to write an infertility declaration and share it with them. This declaration is a combination of natural insights—that which we know needs to happen or can be obstacles—and some scriptures, put into my own words to apply to the situation.

DECLARATION FOR INFERTILITY

I command my body to "be fruitful and multiply" (Gen. 1:28).

I command all blockages to open.

I call forth eggs to release on a timely basis and connect with sperm.

I call forth my uterus to work properly in Jesus' name.

I say, infertility, delay, and lack of conception, leave in Jesus' name.

My bloodline and the bloodline of my children are covered in the blood of Jesus.

I command children to be produced from my womb.

I thank You, Lord, that You "fearfully and wonderfully" make us in our mother's womb (Ps. 139:14). I command miracle-working power to go throughout my womb right now.

I command my husband's male parts to be strong and work properly. Sperm, get to your destination in Jesus' name.

I call forth divine intervention in my womb.

I thank You, Father, that You created life and designed life for my womb.

I thank You that my womb is strong and healthy and can carry several children to full term.

God, as you opened Rachel's womb (Gen. 30:22), I speak to my womb and I say, Be opened by the power of God.

God's Word says the fruit of my womb will be blessed (Luke 1:42). Womb, produce fruit/life!

I come against the enemy and say you will not destroy the destiny of any future child of mine by not producing life. You will not destroy my marriage with dissension and irritation through infertility problems.

There will be no miscarriages or premature deaths in Jesus' name!

No weapon formed against my womb and child-bearing will prosper! (See Isaiah 54:17.)

I call forth life in abundance and that my children will serve the Lord all the days of their lives, in Jesus' mighty and powerful name. Amen! (See John 10:10.)

In writing this declaration I took what I knew in the natural and applied it to this declaration as written statements. I also inserted what I knew of the Scriptures. Now I can give this declaration not to one person but several people and have it bring forth life when it is declared in faith and according to the will of God. Declarations, as you can see, are not just for our benefit, but for the benefit of others. How many women who didn't know how to talk to their body parts and speak things into existence are now empowered in their prayer time?

When writing a natural declaration include what you want to see happen. Call things forth and speak against the obstacles. Decree into the spiritual atmosphere and speak against any doctor's diagnosis. If they say you can't have children, you say you can. If they say your tubes are blocked, you command them to open. If they say the lining on your uterine wall is too thin, you command it to thicken. Speak things into existence, as your Father did when He created the world. Speak it! Say it! Decree it! Believe it! Receive it!

Write a natural declaration for anything you are struggling with. Are you being seduced into a wrong relationship? Write a declaration that says:

I will cast down my flesh and not fulfill its lusts.
I will be faithful and remain pure to my spouse.

> *I command all vain imaginations and false scenarios to go out of my mind in the name of Jesus.*

Take the thoughts, imaginations, and temptations in that area and add to this declaration what you are struggling with. Speak out that you will remain solid in your faith and commitment. Each time you get in your vehicle and drive to work speak it out and declare it!

My daughter believes for something that God told her to come into agreement with. I prophetically wrote a declaration for her that the Spirit of the Lord downloaded to me. I had her write a declaration on the natural knowledge she had on the subject. She prays and declares in her bedroom as led by the Spirit, and each time she gets in her car she uses it as time when she can really declare without other people hearing.

Don't be legalistic in believing that you have to declare out three times a day for the manifestation of your promise. Declare sometimes when you think you should. Make sure it is in a semi-regular, consistent pattern. However, mainly I speak out the declarations that I am called to write as the Spirit of the Lord releases from my spirit. Be obedient. If you hear Him calling you to speak out the declaration, there probably is a reason. My daughter and I talk daily, and there are times when I will tell her I was quickened to declare and pray for her situation and what she is standing in faith for. Each time I tell her I was led to intercede for that request she says that she was also led to declare in that general time frame. The Spirit of God knows what He is doing, and His timing is perfect. When called to declare, do it!

Scriptural Adaptation

Adapting Scripture is a way to start if you don't feel you are creative enough to come up with your own words or if you don't know enough about the subject to know exactly what to bind or loose. Scriptural adaptation is taking a full Scripture verse and using the words in order to make a declaration. You can also use part or the entire verse and put it with several other scriptures to make a declaration. You could make a declaration entirely of scriptures, or you can adapt scriptures and insert them into your natural insight declaration. By combining the two you will have a powerful declaration going back and forth between insight and scriptures that speaks powerfully into the atmosphere.

You can also make a scriptural adaption by using part of a verse or adapting a verse to say what needs to be said in that particular declaration. Please note that we are not twisting or turning Scripture to be manipulative or make it appear the way we want to for our benefit. The end result of the declaration will say the same thing the scripture does, simply in different wording.

The following are some examples of scriptural adaptations:

- *Scripture:* "I can do all things through Christ who strengthens me" (Phil. 4:13).

- *Adaptation:* Christ gives me strength.

- *Scripture:* "Likewise the Spirit also helps in our weaknesses. For we do not know what we should pray for as we ought, but the Spirit Himself makes intercession for us with groanings which cannot be uttered" (Rom. 8:26).

- *Adaptation:* In my weakness the Holy Spirit makes intercession for me.

- *Scripture:* "So the churches were strengthened in the faith, and increased in number daily" (Acts 16:5).

- *Adaptation:* I call forth my church to increase and be strengthened in faith.

You can declare out the entire verse, but it is easier to try and memorize an abbreviated verse. It can be more efficient for your circumstance or the prayer meeting or event you are attending to speak out an abbreviated verse and get right to the point. This will enable those attending to have a better understanding in order to agree with you. It is always good, though, to read and speak the entire scripture aloud in your personal devotional time.

Scriptural declarations and all other declarations can be for personal growth or pruning. They don't just have to be for calling things forth, for what we want or need, or for binding and destroying the spirit realm. God loves it when His children desire to get closer to Him. Some of the declarations I have used to invite the Holy Spirit in to reveal those things that I need revealed and to protect me from against sinning are the following:

PROTECTION AGAINST SIN AND INVITATION FOR DELIVERANCE

"Let not the foot of pride come against me, And let not the hand of the wicked drive me away" (Ps. 36:11).

"Deliver me from all my transgressions" (Ps. 39:8).

> *"Set a guard, O LORD, over my mouth; Keep watch over the door of my lips. Do not incline my heart to any evil thing"* (Ps. 141:3-4).

> *"Teach me to do Your will"* (Ps. 143:10).

> *"Cleanse me from secret faults"* (Ps. 19:12).

> *"Create in me a clean heart"* (Ps. 51:10).

> *"Wash me thoroughly from my iniquity, And cleanse me from my sin"* (Ps. 51:2).

You can also search the Bible for a specific topic using a word search. If you desire to declare about finances, search for scriptures on prosperity, wealth, poverty, and other topics related to finances. You can search for topics using one word. If you are being plagued with mind-binding spirits, search the Scriptures for what the Bible says about your mind and declare those out, such as:

> *I am renewed in the spirit of my mind (Eph. 4:23).*

> *Let this mind be in me which was also in Christ Jesus (Phil. 2:5).*

> *I set my mind on things above, not on things on the earth (Col. 3:2).*

> *God has not given me a spirit of fear but of power and of love and of a sound mind (2 Tim. 1:7).*

Remember, in Romans 10:17 it says, "Faith comes by hearing, and hearing by the word of God." As we speak out Scripture over our life and circumstances we will feel empowered! We will begin to believe what we speak out, which will increase our faith to receive.

Here are additional powerful Scriptures that we can call forth and declare. As we speak, they will empower us on who we are in Him!

> But you are a chosen generation, a royal priesthood, a holy nation, His own special people, that you may proclaim the praises of Him who called you out of darkness into His marvelous light.
>
> —1 PETER 2:9

> For me, that utterance may be given to me, that I may open my mouth boldly to make known the mystery of the gospel.
>
> —EPHESIANS 6:19

Speaking out Scripture is a powerful tool. And as we speak it out repeatedly we also memorize it, which in turn assists us in storing up an arsenal that we can draw from in a time of need. Write up some scriptural declarations using Scripture that would be helpful for you to memorize. Put them on a sheet in front of your Bible so that as you are reading you can both declare and memorize.

Prophetic Revelation

Writing prophetically is having the Spirit of the Lord download the revelation of what to write into your spirit. When I write prophetically I am sitting down by faith and expecting the Holy Spirit to reveal to me what He wants me to write. I could also be in a time of prayer, worship, or Bible study when I will perceive that the Holy Spirit desires me to transition into declaration writing. As I feel the transition I pick up my pen and journal and start writing the first sentence He is revealing.

Since this is a prophetic flow there are usually no stopping points in my writing. It is flowing out as fast as I can write. I stay in tune and try to capture everything He is speaking to me. I keep writing until the flow stops. In these moments I don't pause or stop or wait for revelation. I don't pray in the spirit or in English either to see if I can stir up more revelation. I trust the Holy Spirit that if He is flowing He will continue to do so, and I don't need to cultivate additional revelation.

I don't want to allow my mind to think about it and get my flesh involved in what He desires to convey. Usually, the message in the prophetic declaration is a message that He wants me to share at a meeting or on social media. Therefore, I desire His words to be as accurate as possible. Occasionally the flow will be so rapid and overwhelming that I will have to pick up my laptop and type it out. If you have to do that, it is OK. You don't have to put it all in a journal. Write in whatever is the best way for you to get down what He is conveying for His people. When you write prophetically you can get downloads for multiple declarations at a time. Just make sure you know the stopping and starting point and keep writing.

Prophetic declarations like these can come at any time. Therefore, always be prepared. It can come sitting at a restaurant with people you are ministering to. It can come in a church service or even just sitting around, relaxing. There have been some times when I have had to grab a journal quickly. Again, keep one around, and always be prepared.

I remember one time when I was speaking to a friend about her daughter's situation. Afterward we went into a time of worship. As I started to worship the Spirit of the Lord came over me, and I ended up prostrating myself before the Lord. All of a sudden I started getting revelation regarding her daughter's situation. I started speaking out loud the revelation I was receiving, and my friend wrote down the points. She then took the points that I was prophetically receiving and wrote them into a declaration. My friend started speaking them out, declaring and decreeing with authority. Each time she did it she got louder and meant it even more.

She declared over this situation diligently for three weeks. She never mentioned anything to her daughter about it. Her daughter contacted her and told her about a decision she was making for the future. It was the very decision that my friend was declaring about. Through my friend's declaring God exposed the truth: Bind and restrict the fear of man. My friend could honestly declare out of her spirit. Neither her flesh nor being a mom ever got involved with trying to control or manipulate the situation. She simply took the revelation I received and acted on it through prayer declarations. The situation changed to be in accordance with God's will without either my friend speaking her opinion or communicating the revelation into the situation to her daughter.

Declarations are powerful and produce fruitful results. All three of our children are on fire for the Lord. However, our daughter struggled for a season with some rebellion and legalism issues. She had the typical teenage attitude, and it was affecting the family environment. She was going to be heading off to college, and we saw the need to do some declaring over her life.

She would leave the house, and on about four occasions my husband and I would go into her room and declare into the spiritual realm and over her life. We would anoint her room and her possessions and declare the truth of God's Word and freedom from bondage over her life. We were serious, and we meant business! It was a few months later when we saw drastic improvement in our daughter's life and spiritual walk with Jesus. She went off to college and made an impact for Christ, standing strong in her beliefs, keeping pure sexually, and continuing to abstain from alcohol and drugs, as always. She wouldn't put herself in a bad situation and even went on an evangelism mission trip, where she shared God's love on the streets and talked about Jesus to kids who were drinking alcohol and partying. She shares her faith and beliefs with everyone in college, and they know whom she serves and what she stands for.

The power of declaration works! So many people are in turmoil over their children and their wayward ways. I can tell you that sometimes we need to keep our mouths shut to people but opened wide and loud to the spirit realm. When you declare by faith in accordance to God's will things can't help but be bound and loosed in the atmosphere.

12
TAKING THE
TERRITORY

S PEAKING POSITIVE AFFIRMATIONS into the spirit realm will bring forth spiritual results. There is power in the words we speak. Therefore, as my ministry team and I travel the United States we bring forth and declare prophetically over regions to break up and loose the grounds of demonic strongholds and call forth the revival fire of God to come in the land.

We began declaring over regions when the Spirit of the Lord led us on our first prophetic journey. Just as Jesus was led out into the wilderness by the Spirit of God, we were led out and guided by the Holy Spirit into an unknown land and journey. Through prayer, the Holy Spirit would call us on prophetic love tours where He would give us dates and a general location to travel to or a final destination where we would end up. We would pack our bags, get in the van, and listen to the Holy Spirit tell us to go left or right and to stop at that city, building, store, or restaurant. He would instruct us to drive around and pray, leading us to a city, park, or national monument, where we would pray and declare over that region.

One of the first major prophetic love tours that my team and I went on led us to Lookout Mountain in Tennessee. He instructed me to go up the mountain and then declare over the states that it overlooks. We went and prayed to the north, south, east, and west. I read scriptures over the states and region, and I blew the shofar over the states. The Spirit instructed me as I declared over the regions that He would open doors for me to minister in those regions. Six short months later I was ministering in North Carolina, and God opened doors in Tennessee, Georgia, and Kentucky. We had actively ministered in four out of the seven states within a couple of years.

On one of our ministry trips where we were first beginning to follow the leading of the Holy Spirit we were traveling to Milwaukee, Wisconsin. We were driving into town when I heard the words, "Go up." I looked in the Bible and found these Scripture verses:

> Look, the LORD your God has set the land before you; *go up* and possess it, as the LORD God of your fathers has spoken to you; do not fear or be discouraged. And every one of you came near to me and said, "Let us send men before us, and let them search out the land for us, and bring back word to us of the way by which we should *go up*, and of the cities into which we shall come."
> —DEUTERONOMY 1:21-22, EMPHASIS ADDED

I felt that we received further instructions to go up physically to a high place in order to know what spiritual place He wanted us to take territory in and declare over.

Therefore, we kept following the Spirit's leading and went up into a tall building from which to overlook the city. As we did this He instructed us where else to go in the city. We declared over each place and location He led us to. The Spirit would show us what was at a particular location and exactly how to pray and declare over that building, waterway, or region.

Co-laboring with the Spirit is effective in declaring and decreeing. As we partner with the Spirit of the Lord He will show us what needs to be released and imparted into that particular region. He will reveal the strongholds and how to abolish such attacks with the powerful and anointed Word of God. The Holy Spirit will give you scriptures to declare over a region, and when those scriptures are spoken over a region it establishes things in that region. Declarative prayer is powerful in establishing things, speaking life, and calling things forth for a particular region.

In Scripture we are told to go up and possess the land. As we declare over the region we possess the land for the kingdom of God. My team and I went up physically. But then through prayers and declarations we went up spiritually. In Milwaukee we found that there was a lot of demonic activity taking place. We were able to take the information the Holy Spirit revealed to us and give a PowerPoint presentation to leaders in the region, who then took it back to their intercessors and shared it with other leaders.

Through this time of going up and discovering what the Spirit wanted to show us in Milwaukee doors were opened for us to minister there. We shared the information with a local leader, who introduced us to another leader. I was invited to his church to release the prophetic anointing and minister to individuals in the congregation. He then continued to pursue our ministry and affirmed what we were prophetically releasing. Not only were we able to prophetically establish and break down spiritual strongholds in that area, but it opened doors to minister in multiple churches. Through ministering in these churches we were able to release the Word of God, prophetically speak into multiple people's lives, bring forth the ministry of deliverance into churches and people's lives, deliver young men from gangs, and equip and encourage ministry leaders and pastors who were in need of physical and emotional healing. Also, through this connection I was able to minister to other prophetic pastors in other states who were in need of affirmation and encouragement.

This all started by the power of declaring and establishing in regions. As a result of a simple instruction from the Lord to go to Milwaukee for forty-eight hours and trust Him for the direction, what we declared for in that place wasn't just for a piece of land but for the very people of God. Subsequent ministry happened in hundreds of lives from the ministry we started in that region.

When declaring over a region there are several tools that we use.

Worship

Worship is a powerful tool. When we travel to different regions as the Spirit leads us we worship in those regions. I bring my iPod and a travel dock and release the praises of His people in that land. Praise and worship changes the atmosphere. Praise plows!

Scripture

When I am declaring to establish a region I always read the Word of God out loud over that region. I have highlighted scripture throughout my Bible and also utilize the Book of Psalms. I will declare the Word of God authoritatively over the region, calling things forth and issuing establishments.

Shofar

The shofar was used in the Old Testament, and I believe shofar blowing is powerful. There are many reasons to blow the shofar. However, when I am blowing the shofar over a region I am believing for people to come to repentance and be delivered. I am proclaiming a call to worship.

Flags

Flags, when waved in purity and a sense of respect, are powerful tools in assistance to igniting revival and release across the land. I use these worship flags, which can also be called prayer flags, when I am in a region. I will put on my iPod, worship, dance, pray, declare, and wave flags over a region, waterway, mountain, or wherever the Holy Spirit is calling me. Each worship flag I have stands for something. Prophetically, colors mean something, and when the colors are prophetically designed on a flag the flag takes on spiritual significance. Therefore, when I wave them it is releasing that thing over the region. I have a blue flag with waves, which releases the living waters of God. I have a Holy Spirit flag called Spirit Wind that is yellow for God's glory, blue for releasing the revelation, green for healing, and red for the blood of Jesus over the land. I also have a white flag with gold that is used for releasing the holiness and purity of the Lord Jesus over the region; the gold represents His deity.

Anointing Oil

I also anoint buildings, the land, and waterways when I am declaring. Anointing oil is symbolic of the Holy Spirit. We anoint governmental buildings, doorways, and whatever the Spirit of God is instructing us to anoint during the time of declaring. We are dedicating that object, the people, or the land to the Lord and calling forth compliance and submission to the people around the object that has been anointed.

PROPHETIC LOVE TOURS

The Spirit of the Lord leads us several times a year to go on prophetic love tours. During these tours we share the love of God on the streets and in retail stores, restaurants, and hotels. During this time we can find ourselves releasing encouraging words and affirming people, ministering to the homeless, or praying and declaring for that region.

Declaring in a region isn't always specifically for revival or to establish that region. It can also be to bring unity into the area or to declare and come against a problem that is occurring. God was faithful in having us plan a trip to Ferguson, Missouri. We had the trip already planned, and then the shooting and riots broke out there. We were there five days after the incident and were already prepared with our hotel reservations. We had been praying for the trip, and now we knew we were going there to declare and decree something over the region. As we went we actually worked and ministered along the outskirts of the area and didn't get into the region where the riots were. However, we discovered the people in these areas were just as affected.

We discovered through being obedient and going where the Spirit led that the slavery case of Dred Scott and his appeal to be set free was held in a courthouse in St. Louis, Missouri, across the street from the hotel we were staying in. The Holy Spirit led us to this courthouse at a particular time, and we happened to meet a group from another church that was there interceding on behalf of the region. We ended up meeting divinely in the bookstore and gathered outside to pray and compare notes on what we had received from the Spirit. At the conclusion of our meeting I was invited to minister that weekend in a church and lead a time of prayer and deliverance. The Holy Spirit gave me revelation on how to break down racism in that region and what to declare over that region. I have included these revelations here. They began by declarations against racism, but I have also adapted them for use as general declarations that you can pray over a region.

Declarations Against Racism

> *I release and loose the forces and powers of darkness of their assignments in this region.*

> *I come against racial discrimination, disunity, tension, conflict, bigotry, and injustice in Jesus' name.*

> *Open the floodgates of unity. We call forth unity instead of disunity.*

> *Save all people from persecution from people inside and outside their race. (See Psalm 7:1.)*

Dispense Your peace and love into the hearts of men.

I annihilate and scatter hatred, evil, and bigotry.

I bind the spirit of hatred and command it to be bound and deactivated by the power of the blood of the Lamb.

I bind the power of darkness involving racial discrimination, racial profiling, injustice, bigotry, and racism.

I say no more disunity, division, or segregation. No more unfairness or injustices. No more wavering.

I command destruction of the strongman of racial discrimination, bigotry, attitudes, and intolerance toward those who have different opinions from oneself.

I silence those who want to cause division and strife.

I bring forth the peacemakers.

I annihilate the strongholds and positions of familiar spirits of racism and injustices from years past. I uproot your perceived legal rights and call forth for you to abort your mission by the blood of the Lamb.

I command racism to end in the name of Jesus!

I call forth all hurts from people's past by a person of another race to be healed in Jesus' name.

I proclaim the enemy will be exposed and removed in and from a person's thinking regarding racism.

I say all thoughts planted about prejudices and injustices by our generational line will be removed in Jesus' name.

I call forth an end to racism, for it to be rooted out by the power of God.

I call forth an establishment on Earth of unity and diversity.

I proclaim divine love will come and unite all races, all nations, all ethnicities, and all diversities into unity and human love.

As Christians we are to love all and be in unity with all people. I believe it is the Father's heart for us all to do our part to break down and bridge the divide that racism causes. Let's all work together to end racism by proclaiming these declarations over every area in our nation—not only where we see tensions rising—because every part of the world is impacted by racism.

Regional Declarations

We loose the noose of criticism over this region.

I command skepticism to be bound, uprooted, and destroyed in Jesus' name.

I cancel demonic activities in the atmospheric realms.

I dispel spirits of suicide, murder, death, and darkness in this region and break their power over this area.

We command the spiritual realm to activate on what we say.

We come against addictions, losses, violence, job loss, PTSD, mental illness, relational issues, and despair that lead to homelessness.

I break demonic barriers between the regions in Jesus' name.

No weapon formed against this region will prosper in the name of Jesus.

Father, give us this region "for Your inheritance, And the ends of the earth for Your possession" (Ps. 2:8).

Surround this region with favor like a shield. (See Psalm 5:12.)

I proclaim this region to exhibit and produce a heavenly calm and stillness implanted by love and unity.

I annihilate the forces of fear, chaos, panic, havoc, disunity, dissension, distraction, murder, suicide, death, and destruction with the blood of Jesus.

I command revival fire to come forth and this land to be set ablaze.

Send forth your lightning in abundance and disperse those in opposition to You and peace and unity.

I call forth conviction for the leaders to come together and work in unity and harmony for the kingdom.

I command a sluggish, critical, and judgmental spirit to be bound and cast out from this region.

I bind anger, hate, rage, and violence and command them to depart from this region.

The spoiler will not come and desensitize this region and abort God's plan for spiritual renewal.

Argumentative principalities in this region, we come together in unison and command you to abort your assignment against this region.

Dissension and disunity, be bound in Jesus' name.

Python spirit, uncoil and loose yourself from this region.

I call forth the sounds of heaven to be released and dispatched with angels going forth to destroy the orders against revival assigned by the enemy.

I call forth the love of God to saturate this region.

His goodness and power shall prevail, and the gates of heaven shall be opened on behalf of this land.

Penetrate this region, God, with the magnificence of Your presence and power. Show Your people by demonstration Your greatness!

We call the backslidden to come back to You.

We call forth the homeless, hurting, desolate, and lonely to come and know You in a real and profound way.

We say the arms of heaven and God's mighty right hand will war on our behalf.

Thunders of heaven will come forth and move the darkness away and will bring forth light.

The rains of heaven will be sent forth to refresh.

After we had declared over Ferguson we saw a dramatic decrease in the violence that was happening. We had the local newspapers delivered to our hotel room each day. The first day we were there the riots were making headlines in the paper. As we stayed, took territory, prayed with another ministry, and declared, we saw these activities cease. In fact, one day we walked out of our hotel room to a group of police officers preparing for an assembly of protestors that was supposed to be held. We talked to them, ministered to them, and asked if we could blow the shofar in the park. They agreed to let us. We blew the shofar and declared. The assembly had a few calm people but never materialized, praise God! Glory to Him for answered prayers and the power of declaring and decreeing over a territory and taking authority in the name of Jesus. Perhaps someday the Holy Spirit will allow me to know how many arrests didn't happen that day and how many police officers or citizens didn't get hurt because of the power of declaring through prayer.

The Lord tells us in His Word to go and possess the land. *Possess* is an action word. How can we possess a land if we don't speak out and declare for that land? In Noah Webster's 1828 dictionary the word *possess* is defined as "to seize, to gain, to obtain the occupation."[1] In the Old Testament, when people had to fight to possess the land they had to do so in a natural/physical sense. They had to go to war and battle and fight for the land. They had to get physically involved, which also made them get emotionally involved. Without getting their head in the game through emotional commitment, how could they be sold out to committing to the battle they were in? Declaring over a place is not fleshy, but it does require the investment of our emotional energies; getting our head in the game, so to speak, requires commitment, as any battle would. The word *seize* in Webster's dictionary means "to use legal or official power to take (something); to get or take (something) in a forceful, sudden, or violent way; and to attack and take control of (a place) by force or violence." The force and violence by which we act today to take possession is through the power of prayer.

We know in the Bible that there is a spiritual and natural correlation and that what happens in one happens in the other. We don't fight in the physical.

> For though we walk in the flesh, we do not war according to the flesh. For the weapons of our warfare are not carnal but mighty in God for pulling down strongholds, casting down arguments and every high thing that exalts itself against the knowledge of God, bringing every thought into captivity to the obedience of Christ.
> —2 Corinthians 10:3-5

> Finally, my brethren, be strong in the Lord and in the power of His might. Put on the whole armor of God, that you may be able to stand against the wiles of the devil. For we do not wrestle against flesh and blood, but against principalities, against powers, against the rulers of the darkness of this age, against spiritual hosts of wickedness in the heavenly places. Therefore take up the whole armor of God, that you may be able to withstand in the evil day, and having done all, to stand. Stand therefore, having girded your waist with truth, having put on the breastplate of righteousness, and having shod your feet with the preparation of the gospel of peace; above all, taking the shield of faith with which you will be able to quench all the fiery darts of the wicked one. And take the helmet of salvation, and the sword of the Spirit, which is the word of God; praying always with all prayer and supplication in the Spirit, being

watchful to this end with all perseverance and
supplication for all the saints.
—Ephesians 6:10-18

Our fight is through the power of prayer and
supplication. Prayer is a powerful tool in destroying the
enemy's strongholds and establishing regions.

In order to establish regions, sometimes the Spirit of
God will call you to go into that region. As you go in you
are taking a physical action with your body and aligning
it with the spiritual action of prayer and an emotional
action of the soul (your mind, will, and emotions). You
are activating your heart and mind, being prepared and
ready to be obedient and take a physical, prophetic stance
to coincide with the spiritual stance of prayer you are
taking for that region.

Let's look at our experience in Milwaukee in terms
of the steps in the process of declaring for a region. The
foundation was our team's readiness to receive direction
from the Lord and willingness to set out. When God told
my team to go up, we were already in the van awaiting our
instructions, quite literally.

> Look, the Lord your God has set the land
> before you; go up and possess it, as the Lord
> God of your fathers has spoken to you; do not
> fear or be discouraged.
> —Deuteronomy 1:21

One we arrived we continued to seek specific direction,
so we started by finding a spot of high altitude where we
could survey the region and proclaim and decree over
the area. We used a combination of spiritual warfare
prayer, declarations and decrees, and prayer flags in this

spot and others, as directed by the Holy Spirit. Once we came down from the high place we continued our prayer and declarations and remained sensitive to listen to and act on the direction of the Spirit, and as a result the land opened up to us, and we ended up ministering in several churches in that state for years. We are still preaching there when called upon.

> But I have said to you, "You shall inherit their land, and I will give it to you to possess, a land flowing with milk and honey." I am the LORD your God, who has separated you from the peoples.
> —LEVITICUS 20:24

> See, I have set the land before you; go in and possess the land which the LORD swore to your fathers—to Abraham, Isaac, and Jacob—to give to them and their descendants after them.
> —DEUTERONOMY 1:8

> And it shall be, when you come into the land which the LORD your God is giving you as an inheritance, and you possess it and dwell in it.
> —DEUTERONOMY 26:1

> Then the LORD your God will bring you to the land which your fathers possessed, and you shall possess it. He will prosper you and multiply you more than your fathers.
> —DEUTERONOMY 30:5

THE PRAYER OF JABEZ

Years ago, the *Prayer of Jabez* book by Bruce Wilkinson was very popular. People all over the United States were praying this prayer and reading the book. The book was based on the Scripture in 1 Chronicles in which Jabez declared as a petition to God: "And Jabez called on the God of Israel saying, 'Oh, that You would bless me indeed, and enlarge my territory, that Your hand would be with me, and that You would keep me from evil, that I may not cause pain!' So God granted him what he requested" (1 Chron. 4:10). He prayed and called out to God in the form of a declaration. His petition—phrased in a powerful declaration—was answered, and God expanded his territory. The book may have passed its season or been a fad, but the authoritative Word of God does not grow old or fade away. The same powerful prayer that people prayed years ago can still be prayed today. It is the Word of God that does not fail and does expand borders. Our nation needs revival. Think of the revival that can manifest if we all prayed to expand our borders.

God instructs us to ask of Him. "Ask of Me, and I will give You The nations for Your inheritance, And the ends of the earth for Your possession" (Ps. 2:8). He invites us to ask. We ask through prayer. *To ask* means "to make a request." In this case we need to make a request in a declaration by claiming, commanding, and calling forth that which we know is His will to establish, which is the kingdom of God here on Earth.

We can also declare and take the territory in our homes. One of the ways to do this is by anointing our homes and doorposts with oil and praying and declaring Scriptures over our home. We know that in the Bible putting blood on the doorposts protected the Israelites.

> And you shall take a bunch of hyssop, dip it in
> the blood that is in the basin, and strike the

> lintel and the two doorposts with the blood that is in the basin. And none of you shall go out of the door of his house until morning. For the LORD will pass through to strike the Egyptians; and when He sees the blood on the lintel and on the two doorposts, the LORD will pass over the door and not allow the destroyer to come into your houses to strike you.
>
> —EXODUS 12:22-23

We obviously don't want to put blood on our doorposts, but we can anoint them with oil, write Scripture on our doorposts, and declare Scripture verbally in our home. Declare and plead the blood of Jesus over your home, because there is power in the blood.

Praying and protecting our home ensures that the Lord builds it and is Lord of it.

> Unless the LORD builds the house, They labor in vain who build it; Unless the LORD guards the city, The watchman stays awake in vain.
>
> —PSALM 127:1

Declare over your home, "No weapon formed against you shall prosper" (Isa. 54:17). Speak life into each room and declare to protect your home and call forth good things. Declare things such as:

I call forth good conversations in our dining room.

I speak sweet sleep at night, uninterrupted, and for good, prophetic dreams.

I proclaim everything that is watched on the TV and Internet is edifying.

I say our appliances will work and last a long time.

I declare that our home will be established for the Lord and that everyone who enters will be saturated in His presence and feel His love.

Speaking positive confessions over and over in your home can change the atmosphere of your home. Think about how it contaminates the atmosphere of your home when one person is upset or angry; other people can get tense. Now, the opposite can happen when you speak out positive scriptures and declarations. It can and will fill your home with faith and peace. When you speak out in and over your home you are also claiming and taking territory for the Lord, because you are speaking into your family's life and into the lives of those who enter your home.

What do you need to declare over your home? Write a list. Write a declaration and spend some time in prayer covering, protecting, and calling forth every good and perfect thing for your home and family.

13
AUDIBLE
INSTRUCTIONS

DAVID WAS A man after God's own heart. David conversed with God and sought to please God. We know David relied upon the Lord for many things, and we know His relationship with God was close. We cannot have a close relationship with someone if we don't talk to and communicate with them. Relationships require time and investment, and David enjoyed spending time with God.

We can get an idea of David's relationship with God when we look at and read the Book of Psalms. The psalms are filled with intimate times that David had with the Lord. Oh, how he must have been filled with sweet pleasures communing that closely with our Creator. I know I too enjoy those sweet moments of fellowship with the Lord.

However, just like a relationship in the natural takes two people talking back and forth, our Lord desires us to speak to Him, and then He can speak back to us spirit to Spirit, communicating with us those special things that we long to hear or even an answer to prayer.

We know that there were also struggles and challenges that David faced. There were times when David had to cry out to God in distress and in times of spiritual warfare. We know there were several occasions when Saul desired to take David's life. What would those conversations with God have been like? How did they communicate? Was it Spirit to spirit, or did David hear God speak audibly to him? How did God respond to David's pleas? What did it look like when He responded to his adoration with affection?

When we are in a spiritual battle and need to pray, crying out to God with prayers in our mind somehow doesn't seem quite strong enough. How can we truly express in our mind the desperation we are in for God to answer our prayer? Think about when we need to get our point across to a person or really need their help. Can a silent conversation convey our point? Of course not! We need to verbally communicate with that person. I believe that is what David has modeled in the Bible for us, to verbally communicate with God.

What seems more effective in your prayer time? Thinking, "God help me. You know my situation. You know I need Your intervention." Or speaking out loud, "*God, help me!* God, I am desperate for You to show me the strategy to get this spiritual warfare to cease. Jesus, intervene for me! Give me divine strategies. Heavenly Father, I call out to You. *Save me!*"

I believe that sometimes we can't get our prayers answered because we think we are praying in our spirit when we are truly thinking about our situation in our mind, pondering it instead of praying about it. I believe that is why it is good to decree and declare our prayers out loud—so that we get our mind busy and don't think about it. We take action and pray about it instead.

When I look at David and the distresses he must have been under I don't think a silent conversation would have cut it. What about Jesus when He prayed so hard in the garden that He sweat blood? Do you really think that praying in His mind, connecting only in spirit, would have gotten the job done? Absolutely not! He was in anguish, pleading with His Father. That kind of prayer could have only been done verbally, out loud, spoken out, and I'm sure there must have been a raised voice in there somewhere. Do you think He said in a mousy way, "Father, take this cup from Me?" or do you think He cried out with anguish, stress, grief, confidence, and desperation, *"Father! Take this cup from Me!"*

When we study about David in the Book of 2 Samuel, we discover many verbal action words referring to His prayer life, words such as *spoke, call upon, cried out, cry,* and *said.* These are all action words, words that he had to speak. To speak you need to open your mouth, move your lips and tongue, and activate your vocal cords and voice box. These are actions that we have to take, like David, and when we exercise all of these communication skills they have power and obtain great results.

When David spoke a song it was a prayer, a declaration of faith. He was stating who his God is but also the delivering power that comes from his God. But what I love about 2 Samuel 22 is how God responded to David's plea in distress. I think many times that when we pray in our mind we are thinking about our problems and getting stuck in a direction that is unfruitful and unprofitable. We can't effectively convey to God what is in our heart. But, when David cried out to God He responded powerfully!

Right at the beginning of 2 Samuel 22 we discover the words *spoke, said* and *call upon*:

> Then David spoke to the LORD the words of this
> song, on the day when the LORD had delivered
> him from the hand of all his enemies, and from
> the hand of Saul. And he said: "The LORD is
> my rock and my fortress and my deliverer;
> The God of my strength, in whom I will trust;
> My shield and the horn of my salvation, My
> stronghold and my refuge; My Savior, You save
> me from violence. I will call upon the LORD,
> who is worthy to be praised; So shall I be saved
> from my enemies.
>
> —2 SAMUEL 22:1-4

David spoke to the Lord. He didn't think or communicate in his thoughts. He spoke.

Furthermore, in the day of deliverance he verbally declared out loud who the Lord is, his Rock, Fortress, and Deliverer. He declared Him as the God of his strength and declared his trust for Him. Some of us would do well to verbally declare out loud that God is our trust. I know I have had to do it several times in the past.

David continued to praise the Lord with his words. He declared God as a stronghold, refuge, and Savior. He proceeded to acknowledge that the Lord saves him from violence. These words are powerful!

I believe some of our situations would change if we declared out loud who God is or should be to us instead of us thinking and pondering in our minds what is not happening. When we declare out who God is we are taking our focus off of our problems and the victim mentality that could be attacking us and putting it on who God is and the victory that we have in Him. It can take us from sulking to rejoicing in a minute.

David declared out the Lord as a refuge, a place of rest, and retreat. Speaking these words will bring us life. It will bring us to a place of rest and retreat, knowing that God protects us, since He is our shield. He is our safety, our place of solace. As we speak out who the Lord is, it comes back into our ears, into our soul, and into our spirit man and builds us up. As we hear those words we start to believe them, and they become part of us as we live them out.

David continued to say that he would call upon the Lord, who is worthy to be praised (v. 4). "I will call upon" are action words. He is stating that when he calls upon the Lord he will be saved. He is doing his part, so therefore God can respond. David got up and called upon God. And God responded by saving David, which is preserving him, helping him, rescuing him, defending him, and delivering him.

We could all use God to save us in a particular situation, but first we need to do our part as David did and call upon the Lord, verbally, out loud. We need not just to think it but do it, like the Nike slogan, Just do it! Sometimes we need to just do it instead of thinking about it.

When David was in distress he prayed. Often when we are in distress we don't know how to pray. In times like those I think we need a list of simple declarations that we can speak out so that we know what to pray and can declare them out in the natural until the spiritual and the natural connect via the Holy Spirit. In David's distress he cried out to God in a pivotal time: "In my distress, I called upon the LORD, And cried out to my God; He heard my voice from His temple, And my cry entered His ears" (2 Sam. 22:7). He called upon the Lord and cried out to his God. We need not just to be reading the Word of God, but like David, we need to be applying the very principles and instructions of the Word of God to our lives.

I love 2 Samuel 22:7 because of all the verbs it contains and actions David took. He called upon and cried out to our God. But look how God responded: God heard David's voice from His temple, and David's cry entered God's ears. God heard David. David's cry entered God's ears. It wasn't David connecting with the very Spirit of God and his spirit; it was David's verbal plea and outcry entering the very temple of God. David cried out, and God listened. We could say that God was obedient and heard, responded, and acted on David's petition. He understood David's cry, not his thoughts but the very words David spoke. This is a prime example of how we should be praying—verbally, out loud, declaring! Hallelujah! Thank You, Lord!

David spoke, and God responded.

> Then the earth shook and trembled; The foundations of heaven quaked and were shaken Because He was angry. Smoke went up from His nostrils, And devouring fire from His mouth; Coals were kindled by it. He bowed the heavens also, and came down With darkness under His feet. He rode upon a cherub, and flew; And He was seen upon the wings of the wind. He made darkness canopies around Him, Dark waters and thick clouds of the skies. From the brightness before Him Coals of fire were kindled. "The Lord thundered from heaven, And the Most High uttered His voice. He sent out arrows and scattered them; Lightning bolts, and He vanquished them. Then the channels of the sea were seen, The foundations of the world were uncovered, At the rebuke of the

Lord, At the blast of the breath of His nostrils.
"He sent from above, He took me, He drew me
out of many waters. He delivered me from my
strong enemy, From those who hated me; For
they were too strong for me. They confronted
me in the day of my calamity, But the Lord
was my support. He also brought me out into
a broad place; He delivered me because He
delighted in me.

—2 SAMUEL 22:8-20

God responded to David's declaration, and the earth
shook and trembled. God released holy, righteous anger,
which led to action. God was moved by David's prayer.
God was agitated. David called upon God and stirred God
to action. I love that! We can pray and declare in such a
way that we stir and call God to action.

Here David called and cried out. He activated his
physical body by activating his voice, his vocal cords.
He was emotionally involved because he cried out. God
responded with breath coming out of His nostrils,
representing the physical, and holy, righteous anger,
representing His emotions and the Spirit part of Him.
God's very being was affected and responded to David's
verbal yet physical plea because David got his physical body
involved when he spoke, cried out, and called out. From
God's nostrils came His breath (v. 9). I love this. You see,
when Jesus ministered He got His entire being involved.
He touched people to represent His physical body. Jesus
had compassion on people, which involved emotions. And
we know that He operated in the spirit to represent the
Spirit. He involved every aspect of His being.

I believe that when we decree and declare we too need
to get our physical being active. We need to get out of

our chair and out of our bed and walk the floor, kneel in adoration and desperation, or prostrate ourselves before the Lord and cry out to Him. I have a hard time believing that we can cry out in desperation and declare by leaning back in our recliner in a comfy position. We need to release the spiritual by activating the natural.

God responded to David by bowing the heavens. Bowing the heavens means that He opened up and stretched out the heavens on David's behalf. We all long to tap into the heavenly. Here is a firm example of how the heavens are rendered open when we cry out and call out to our God. Praise God! Hallelujah for that! It says He "came down With darkness under His feet" (v. 10). All that warfare David was experiencing was under the Lord's feet—the misery, destruction, death, and wickedness: "He bowed the heavens also, and came down With darkness under His feet" (v. 10).

Verse 14 continues, "The Lord thundered from heaven, And the Most High uttered His voice." God conducted the warfare for David: "He sent out arrows and scattered them; Lightning bolts, and He vanquished them" (v. 15). He sent out and loosed arrows and scattered them. He sent forth lightning bolts and disturbed, destroyed, consumed, and crushed the enemy.

Then the ultimate victory is that because of David's desperate plea God rescued Him.

> He sent from above, He took me, He drew me out of many waters. He delivered me from my strong enemy, From those who hated me; For they were too strong for me.
>
> —2 Samuel 22:17-18

God was strong and intervened when David was weak.

There is so much that came out of this time of distress, including how David praised and declared who the Lord is and what the Lord did for Him. What David was doing was prophesying over himself with words of adoration for the Lord and for what the Lord would do for him. David spoke it into existence at the praise of his lips and in the confidence of who his God is.

When we continue to look at David and his pleas in the psalms and study some of the definitions of the words he uses we can get a deeper revelation. When studying the Bible I enjoy looking up the definitions in *Strong's Concordance* or a dictionary in order to pull out the full meaning and context.

In Psalm 55:1-2 it says, "Give ear to my prayer, O God, And do not hide Yourself from my supplication. Attend to me, and hear me; I am restless in my complaint, and moan noisily." The word *prayer* here is intercession or supplication. It refers to a song. Songs are meant to be sung out loud.[1] The word *complaint* is an indication of utterance, babbling, communication, talk, and prayer.[2] The word *noise* is defined as "an uproar, or to agitate greatly."[3] We should be praying aggressively!

David continues with Psalm 55:16-17: "As for me, I will call upon God, And the LORD shall save me. Evening and morning and at noon I will pray, and cry aloud, And He shall hear my voice." I love the definition of *call*, which is "to announce, preach, and proclaim."[4] How differently we would pray if we thought about calling upon God as preaching! When we look at the word *pray* we see that it means "to converse with oneself and hence aloud."[5] It is also described as "to utter, complain, and declare."[6] I love how the very Bible and the deeper meaning of Scripture can verify that we need to be praying aloud and declaring!

The words *cry aloud* are defined as "to make a loud sound, war, moan, be moved, and make a noise."[7] When praying we should be praying so fervently that all of heaven hears!

We can continue to see in the Book of Psalms how David prophesied over himself and also prophesied what God brought forth and did.

> Give ear to my words, O LORD, Consider my meditation. Give heed to the voice of my cry, My King and my God, For to You I will pray. My voice You shall hear in the morning, O LORD; In the morning I will direct it to You, And I will look up. For You are not a God who takes pleasure in wickedness, Nor shall evil dwell with You. The boastful shall not stand in Your sight; You hate all workers of iniquity. You shall destroy those who speak falsehood; The LORD abhors the bloodthirsty and deceitful man. But as for me, I will come into Your house in the multitude of Your mercy; In fear of You I will worship toward Your holy temple. Lead me, O LORD, in Your righteousness because of my enemies; Make Your way straight before my face. For there is no faithfulness in their mouth; Their inward part is destruction; Their throat is an open tomb; They flatter with their tongue. Pronounce them guilty, O God! Let them fall by their own counsels; Cast them out in the multitude of their transgressions, For they have rebelled against You. But let all those rejoice who put their trust in You; Let them ever shout for joy, because You defend them; Let those also who love Your name Be joyful in You. For You,

O L<small>ORD</small>, will bless the righteous; With favor
You will surround him as with a shield.

—P<small>SALM</small> 5:1-12

Again, David is petitioning the Lord to give ear to
his words. David is inquiring of the Lord, but more so
he is saying, "Hear me. Hear my words." Not, "Hear my
thoughts." Not, "Connect with me Spirit to spirit," but,
"Hear my words." He is petitioning the Lord to heed his
voice and his cry, which again, is a verbal, physical exercise,
with his cry being an out-loud movement.

> L<small>ORD</small>, how they have increased who trouble
> me! Many are they who rise up against me.
> Many are they who say of me, "There is no help
> for him in God." Selah But You, O L<small>ORD</small>, are
> a shield for me, My glory and the One who
> lifts up my head. I cried to the L<small>ORD</small> with my
> voice, And He heard me from His holy hill.
> Selah I lay down and slept; I awoke, for the
> L<small>ORD</small> sustained me. I will not be afraid of ten
> thousands of people Who have set themselves
> against me all around. Arise, O L<small>ORD</small>; Save me,
> O my God! For You have struck all my enemies
> on the cheekbone; You have broken the teeth
> of the ungodly. Salvation belongs to the L<small>ORD</small>.
> Your blessing is upon Your people. Selah
>
> —P<small>SALM</small> 3:1-8

David has shown us the power of declaring, speaking
out who the Lord is. He has written many chapters and
verses full of declarations that we can speak out at any
time. He has shown us the power of using our voice. He
has also shown us that the Lord hears from His temple
and how to cry out to our God. Now the final question is,

What are you going to do about it in order to activate your faith, combat spiritual warfare, call forth the blessings of God, and change your situation?

EPILOGUE

CLOSING PROPHETIC DECLARATION

I establish what you have learned here will grow and be nourished by the Word of God.

I speak over your life and call forth your prophetic destiny.

I proclaim that the enemy will not come to steal, kill, or destroy one word of what you speak out.

I declare that you will be firmly rooted and established in the Word of God and the message from God on declaring.

I call forth the heavens to open on your behalf and for everything you speak according to the will of God to manifest on Earth.

I command any confusion, doubt, or unbelief to leave you regarding speaking out establishments and statements in order to create and build things for the kingdom.

I say you will be prosperous in whatever you set your mind, heart, and mouth to.

I decree you will take your authority and change your circumstances, in Jesus' name.

NOTES

CHAPTER 6: SCRIPTURES WERE MEANT TO BE READ

1.   Theodore Geisel, *Green Eggs and Ham* (New York: Random House, 1960).

CHAPTER 7: LORD, YOU SAID IF I ASK

1.   *Strong's Exhaustive Bible Concordance Online*, accessed at *e-Sword*, http://www.e-sword.net/, February 14, 2017, s.v. "H3427."
2.   Finis Jennings Dake, *The Dake Annotated Reference Bible*, KJV (Lawrenceville, GA: Dake Publishing, 2013), s.v. "Psalm 91" and *"yashab."*
3.   *Strong's Exhaustive Bible Concordance Online*, s.v. "H3885."
4.   Ibid., s.v. "H5526."

CHAPTER 10: DEFINING YOUR WORDS

1.   Noah Webster, *An American Dictionary of the English Language, 1828 edition*, available at *WebstersDictionary1828.com*, February 7, 2017, s.v. "call."
2.   Ibid.
3.   Ibid., s.v. "command."
4.   Ibid., s.v. "instruction."
5.   Ibid., s.v. "order."
6.   Ibid., s.v. "power."
7.   Ibid., s.v. "speak."
8.   Ibid., s.v. "strength."
9.   Unless otherwise noted, all of the definitions in this section are quoted from the *Merriam-Webster Dictionary Online*, www.merriam-webster.com.
10.   The *Merriam-Webster Online Dictionary* defines *to confine* as "to hold within a location; to keep within limits." See *Merriam-Webster Online Dictionary*, Merriam-Webster Incorporated, February 8, 2017, s.v. "confine."

CHAPTER 12: TAKING THE TERRITORY

1.   Webster, *An American Dictionary of the English Language, 1828 edition*, s.v. possess."

CHAPTER 13: AUDIBLE INSTRUCTIONS

1.   *Strong's Exhaustive Bible Concordance Online*, s.v. "H8605."

2.   Ibid., s.v. "H7879."

3.   Ibid., s.v. "H1949."

4.   Ibid., s.v. "H7121."

5.   Ibid., s.v. "7878."

6.   Ibid.

7.   Ibid., s.v. "H1993."

ABOUT THE AUTHOR

Kathy DeGraw is the founder and president of DeGraw Ministries, a prophetic healing and deliverance ministry releasing the love and power of God. She travels internationally, imparting into believers and igniting them to release their full potential.

She is passionate about empowering people to serve and love God and people in every action. She brings her *Be Love* prophetic tours around the US, ministering through street evangelism and empowering believers to release the prophetic and be love.

Kathy is the author of *Flesh, Satan or God, Time to Set the Captives Free, Warfare Declarations, A Worship-Woven Life*, and *The Sky's the Limit*. She has written a four-day deliverance school and three-day inner healing school with which she travels the US empowering churches and ministries to start their own healing and freedom ministry.

She is passionate about bridging the divide of racism through her corporation, Change Into Colorless. Her desire is to bring forth healing, unity, and love around the world through educating people on forgiveness and racial issues.

Kathy is married to her best friend, Pastor Ron DeGraw. Together they co-pastor Ruach Ha'Kodesh Apostolic Empowerment Center. She is mom to three adult children, Dillon, Amber, and Lauren. They reside in Grandville, Michigan.

ADDITIONAL BOOKS BY KATHY DEGRAW

A Worship Woven Life (Tate Publishing, 2014)

Time to Set the Captives Free (Tate Publishing, 2014)

Flesh, Satan, or God (Tate Publishing, 2014)

The Sky's the Limit (CSS Publishing, 2008)

Warfare Declarations (K Publishing, 2017)

Baptism of Fire and Power (K Publishing, 2017)

CONTACT THE AUTHOR

To be in touch with Kathy, follow her on Facebook, YouTube, or Twitter @Kathy DeGraw.

To inquire about booking Kathy for a speaking engagement, contact:

DeGraw Ministries

P.O. Box 65

Grandville, MI 49468

Website: www.degrawministries.org

E-mail: admin@degrawministries.org